One Island, Many Voices

❖ ❖ ❖

One Island, Many Voices

Conversations with Cuban-American Writers

Eduardo R. del Rio

The University of Arizona Press
Tucson

The University of Arizona Press
© 2008 The Arizona Board of Regents
All rights reserved

Library of Congress Cataloging-in-Publication Data
appear on the last printed page of this book.

Publication of this book is made possible in part by
the proceeds of a permanent endowment created with
the assistance of a Challenge Grant from the National
Endowment for the Humanities, a federal agency.

Manufactured in the United States of America on acid-free,
archival-quality paper containing a minimum of 30% post-consumer
waste and processed chlorine free.

13   12   11   10   09   08   6   5   4   3   2   1

Unless otherwise noted, photographs were taken by the author.

For my mother, Candida,
whose unfulfilled dream was to return
to Havana, and for my daughter, Alexis,
who will hopefully someday
realize that dream.

.:.

⁂ ⁂ ⁂

Contents

❖ ❖ ❖

Acknowledgments

I would like to thank the National Endowment for the Humanities for awarding me a Faculty Research Grant that made it possible to travel to the homes of these writers and interview them in person. I would also like to express my gratitude to The University of Texas at Brownsville for allowing me the time to work on this project. In particular, Dr. Chip Dameron, then Dean of the College of Liberal Arts, made sure that the red tape associated with the grant and my leave of absence would not interrupt my research. Prof. Bill Harris, chairman of the English Department, also was instrumental in this effort. I would also like to thank my editor, Patricia Rosas, for her tireless attention to detail during the final stages of manuscript preparation. Most importantly, I want to thank the twelve writers who were gracious enough to accept my invitation to participate in this project. I had known them only through words on a page, but now I feel that I've made lasting friendships.

Preface

Several years ago, I was asked by a literary journal to review a book of interviews with Puerto Rican writers. Although it was not her main goal, the author of that collection seemed to be establishing a canon of writers from that Caribbean nation. As I finished writing the review, it occurred to me that it would be interesting, and professionally benefi-cial, to compile a collection of interviews with Cuban-American writers. Therefore, when I finally undertook the project a few years later, it was spurred more by an academic interest than a personal one. I was also well aware of the danger inherent in belonging to the group that one is studying, but despite my Cuban origin, I was confident that I could remain unbiased.

My initial contact with each author via e-mail or letter was promptly answered, and all the authors were not just interested in the project but were also pleasant and extremely engaging. I suppose I expected some of them to respond, as some creative people are wont to do, with either condescension or outright irritation. Because I wanted to give the reader a sense of each writer's personality, I decided I would interview each of them face to face. They all welcomed me into their homes or the places they work, and they seemed genuinely interested in not just getting to know the project better, but getting to know me, as well. With some, I established an instant connection, and a genuine friendship seemed to emerge.

The questions and answers reproduced in this book focus on the lives and work of twelve Cuban-American writers. There is no bias in my selection of these particular authors, since any objective analysis would conclude that the authors gathered in this collection represent the most significant literary and critical voices in Cuban-American studies today. Over the course of the two-and-a-half years that it has taken to write the book, however, I have come to accept that my feelings about these people are biased. Perhaps our mutual experience of living as exiles colors my view. Perhaps my growing interest and affection for the literature that mirrors my life has skewed my perception. I am confident, however, that any reader, regardless of his or her background, will more fully appreciate the work of the men and women in this book after getting to know them as I know them. I have tried to share that knowledge with the reader by providing a glimpse into the writing, the sensibilities, and the passions of twelve gifted authors.

One Island, Many Voices

✻ ✻ ✻

Introduction

In her 1988 book on Cuban-American writers, Carolina Hospital includes
selections by authors whose primary language is Spanish but who write
poetry and prose in their adopted tongue. Because employing English to
write about the Cuban-American experience was, in her estimation, a new
phenomenon, she subtitled the book *Los Atrevidos* (The Daring Ones).[1]
In 1999, Pamela Maria Smorkaloff attempted to bridge the literary and
linguistic gap between Cuba and the United States in her *Cuban Writers
on and off the Island*.[2] In the final section of that book, for instance,
Smorkaloff examines the narrative fiction of Cuban-American authors,
such as Achy Obejas and Roberto Fernández, as part of her overall analysis of Latino literature. These are only two of the many recent publications that focus on Latino literature, in general, and Cuban-American
writers, in particular, and it indicates a growing interest in this academic
field. None of these publications, however, allow the writers themselves to
explore the issue of dual identity and linguistic difference inherent in their
works. This book is designed to rectify that glaring omission.

Several years ago, Juan Bruce-Novoa published a much-acclaimed
book of interviews with Chicano writers,[3] and more recently, Carmen
Dolores Hernández did the same with their Puerto Rican counterparts.[4]
One Island, Many Voices presents a series of interviews with some of
the most distinguished Cuban-American writers in the United States. It
is designed to explore some the issues prevalent in the field of Cuban-
American literature. These twelve well-known Cuban-American authors
are working in a wide range of genres, including poetry, fiction, and
drama. The book also incorporates a broad array of viewpoints, including the somewhat marginalized but highly significant perspective of gay
writers. The authors selected for this study were chosen based both on
their prominence and on several guidelines that I believe define Cuban-
American literature.

First, the Cuban-American writers in this collection were born in Cuba but have lived in the United States for most of their lives. This is crucial because it means the writer's artistic consciousness has been affected by the sounds, images, and experiences of American life. Second, the works of these Cuban-American writers contain similar characteristics, including an attention to family, a concern for home, an interest in historical formulations, and a focus on cultural components, such as music, food, and religion. Additionally, their works deal with matters of identity formation, appropriation, and determination.

A sense of duality regarding the English language is another trait of Cuban-American literature that is prominent in the works of these twelve writers. For some of them, Spanish may be a mere memory or something experienced sporadically through familial bonds. Others, however, are more at home in the Spanish language, and English thus represents a direct confrontation with a new and confusing tongue. For all of these writers, however, their linguistic consciousness includes a sense of both languages. Because of this duality, the body of Cuban-American writers' works is written primarily in English, as they seek to express this conflict in the language that is the embodiment of it.

Finally, and most significantly, Cuban-American writers are exiles, and their literature reflects the sense of loss associated with the forced departure from their homeland. Although these twelve authors have had their artistic consciousness shaped by American life, it has also unarguably been shaped by their exilic experience and the memory of Cuba.

The criteria employed to select these twelve writers served as a paradigm to formulate questions that would explore the creative process as it pertains to Cuban-American literature. The questions were chosen with several goals in mind. First, the interviews are designed to establish what makes Cuban-American literature distinctive. There are clear similarities between Cuban-American literature and its Mexican-American and Puerto Rican counterparts. All these groups share the use of the Spanish language, and they collectively trace their heritage to indigenous and African roots. Perhaps the most important bond, however, is related to the concept of identity. All three groups have a shared past of having been and, some argue, continuing to be (as in the case of Puerto Rico) a colonized and oppressed people. Because of this, all three groups have developed a strong nationalistic sense, while at the same time feeling the need to be accepted by the people in their adopted home. The interviews focus on this dimension of Cuban-American literature in order to determine how it differs from other Latino writings. Secondly, the interviews explore the theoretical aspects of the literature, including such issues as hyphenation, labeling, gender, and sexuality. In her seminal work on this topic, *Cuban-American Literature of Exile*,[5] Isabel Alvarez-Borland has explored these issues by focusing on matters that are specific to individual authors, while still framing the discussion in terms of Cuban-American literature. Her examination of the work of Achy Obejas, for instance, concentrates on matters of sexual identity, but only as it is relevant to the broader issue of the Cuban diaspora. My purpose is similar. The type of question I offered to a writer was designed to elicit a response that examines the unique qualities of that author, without losing the connection to the larger arena of Cuban-American literature. What role does memory play in the novels of Cristina García? How does humor relate to Cuban culture in the work of Roberto Fernández? How are Cuban-American women portrayed in the plays of Dolores Prida? Finally, and perhaps more importantly, because this is ultimately a study in American literature, I wanted to determine how the individual authors perceive their work to be connected, if at all, to the American literary tradition. This is a crucial component designed to contribute to the humanities in both a theoretical and pedagogical manner. In other words, the authors' reflections on this issue will serve both teachers and scholars who might want to explore the similarities in technique and thematic content between a Cuban-American novel and one by Twain, Hemingway, or Faulkner.

In order to lay the groundwork for the connection between Cuban-American literature and the American literary tradition, I begin with a brief survey of Cuban-American literary history. Although we usually think of Cuban literature as the exile literature of the Castro era, the literary connection between the two countries has deep historical roots. Many early exiled writers focused their work on the country they left behind, while they almost entirely ignored their newfound land. Later, the literature, now completely embracing America as its authors' political and economic savior, was a vehicle to castigate Castro's regime. In the last three decades, there has been a definite shift in this two-dimensional portrait, however. Some writers continue to describe the conflict between Cubans and Americans, but they also depict the U.S. economic system as an exploiter of Cuban workers, a subject considered taboo by many earlier writers. Most recently, many Cuban-American authors have further problematized the relationship between Cuba and the United

States by using humor to explore the linguistic and cultural confusion of exile. Additionally, authors have attempted to depict Cuban-Americans' feelings toward the United States as more than a mere dichotomy. This survey will place the interviews that follow in their proper historical context, as these twelve authors reveal their own sense of place within this history.

In addition to the introductory material, each interview is preceded by a biographical sketch. As is traditional, these sketches summarize the author's academic and professional accomplishments. However, part of the book's subtitle, "Conversations," rather than "Interviews," reflects its attempt to humanize each author and make him or her come alive for the reader. Thus, these sketches also reveal characteristics of each writer that are not usually considered in a book of this nature and that may not be evident when one reads their poetry or prose. These personal details, which include such things as appearance, mannerisms, speech patterns, and sense of humor, also help illuminate the conversations that follow.

Finally, a few words must be included here regarding the omission of certain writers. As noted earlier, all of the authors in this book have lived in the United States for a significant period of time, they write extensively in English, but they were born in Cuba. Many critical attempts have been made to establish the parameters of Cuban-American literature. Drawing on sociologist Rubén Rumbaut's labeling of children who were born abroad but educated and raised in the United States as the *one-and-a-half generation*, Gustavo Pérez Firmat applies the term to Cuban-born writers, such as himself. Because of their birthplace, he would identify the writers in this volume as *Cuban-American*, and he distinguishes between them and Cubans, whom he identifies as those individuals who left the island as adults, and *Cuban-Bred* Americans, the U.S.–born children of Cuban exiles.[6]

Isabel Alvarez-Borland also attempts to define Cuban-American literature, and like Pérez Firmat, she includes writers who are members of the one-and-a-half generation and also those she calls Cuban-American *ethnic* writers, second-generation Cubans who "came from Cuba as infants or who were born in the United States to parents of the first exile generation." Alvarez-Borland observes that the literature of these second-generation writers places a greater distance between the writers and the events of the diaspora."[7] Partially relying on these two definitions,[8] I have concluded that the twelve writers included here must be classified as *Cuban-American* writers both because their work is often centered around the diaspora (thus making them ineligible to qualify as *ethnic* writers) and because they were born on the island.

Because of this focus on Cuba as a starting point, at least three talented writers—Oscar Hijuelos, Ana Menéndez, and Richard Blanco[9]— are not included here. Again, Pérez Firmat makes it clear that despite Hijuelos's popular success, particularly his Pulitzer Prize-winning *The Mambo Kings Play Songs of Love*, he lacks a true understanding of Cuban culture. Pérez Firmat asserts that although Hijuelos is "coeval with the Miami one-and-a-halfers, his outlook is . . . much closer to the second generation."[10] In other words, Hijuelos is, in Pérez Firmat's opinion, an American-Bred Cuban, rather than a Cuban-American writer. Ana Menéndez, who was born in Los Angeles to Cuban exiles, also doesn't qualify to be included here based on place of origin. Blanco was born in Spain shortly after his mother arrived there from Cuba, so it is somewhat difficult to label him based on his origins. Moreover, this book focuses not just on place of origin but also on established writers with a significant literary corpus. Leaving aside whether or not Blanco should be considered a Cuban-American writer, he has not yet had the same impact as his fellow poets Ricardo Pau-Llosa and Dionisio Martínez.

Anyone who has ever edited an anthology or collection knows that the process of selection, by definition, involves exclusion. This book, though necessarily excluding some writers, nevertheless presents the reader with twelve authors who not only represent a wide range of genres, but who constitute the core of the Cuban-American literary canon. Although technically all twelve can be classified as part of the one-and-a-half generation,[11] that would do them a great disservice, because placing them under that single rubric might imply that they share the same literary sensibilities and preoccupations. Even though they are all Cuban-American authors and thus share a hyphenated existence, as they speak about their work, it will be evident that we need to look beyond the hyphen to appreciate the uniqueness of each of these gifted writers.

Cuban-American Literature: A Brief Survey

Cuban-American poetry and prose has a rich and varied history. As early as 1823, for instance, a Cuban writer, José María Heredia, fled the island to the United States to avoid imprisonment. Employing two common symbols, the royal palm and the solitary star, Heredia's poetry sharply criticized the Spanish authorities and depicted a Cuba free of Spain's tyrannical grasp. Like Heredia, many other nineteenth-century writers found it impossible to live and write in Cuba, including Cirilo Villaverde and the incomparable José Martí, both of whom also fled to the United States, where they promptly began writing about their homeland. Writing in Spanish, José Martí's poetry reflects his sense of patriotism, and his book of poems *Versos sencillos* (Simple Verses) (1891) echoes the sentiments expressed by Heredia.

The literature of Cuban exiles also established roots early in the twentieth century. Alejo Carpentier, for instance, chose to leave his native land in 1928 after having spent forty days in jail. Carpentier, considered by many as the father of Cuban novelists, has had his works translated into several languages. Although he decided to return home in 1959 to show his support for the revolution, many other Cuban writers, fearing what that revolution might bring, decided to leave. One of the first to seek asylum in the United States was Lino Novas Calvo. Exile renewed Calvo's interest in creative writing, and he produced many stories, most dealing with aspects of pre-revolutionary Cuba. Perhaps the best known Cuban writer of that century, however, is Guillermo Cabrera Infante. After supporting Castro's regime and even serving as Cuba's cultural attaché until 1965, Infante left Cuba never to return. His work has been compared to that of Hemingway and Joyce, and his most successful novel, *Tres tristes tigres* (*Three Trapped Tigers*), employs puns and extensive wordplay in an attempt to faithfully recreate the dialect of Havana in the 1950s, the work's setting. Many of these early exiled writers focused their work on the land they left behind. Often, their texts were replete with nostalgia. For others, their literature served as a vehicle to castigate Castro's regime. Among the latter may be included such writers as Emilio Fernández Camus, Orlando Núñez, and Luis Ricardo Alonso.

In the last three decades of the twentieth century, the focus began to shift away from Cuba and Castro, turning toward a consideration of Cuban exiles' lives in the United States. Celedonio González, beginning with his work *Los primos* (The Cousins) (1971), concentrates on Cuban life and culture in the United States. Later, in *Los cuatro embajadores* (The Four Ambassadors) (1973), González not only examines culture shock and conflict between Cubans and Americans, but he also depicts the United States economic system as an exploiter of Cuban workers. The exile-as-conflict literature is also explored by Matías Montes Huidobro in the award-winning novel *Desterrados al fuego* (Exiled to the Fire). This first-person narrative, told by a husband who has recently arrived in the United States, reveals how he is overwhelmed by the alien culture's requirements. In an almost Chekhovian fashion, the man's failure to adjust results in his spiritual and physical deterioration.

The twelve writers in this collection have further explored the conflictual relationship between Cuba and the United States. Some of them, such as Roberto Fernández, for instance, use humor to explore the linguistic and cultural confusion of exile. Additionally, these authors have attempted to depict Cuban-Americans' feelings toward the United States as more than a simple either/or dichotomy. The work of these twelve writers makes it clear that Cuban-American literature has continued to evolve, and this evolution has helped this body of work integrate more fluidly into the American mainstream.[12] In the interviews, many of the authors express their belief that this process is a central factor in connecting their work to the American literary tradition. Carolina Hospital, for example, explains that when she published her anthology almost twenty years ago, scholars were not sure where to place it within the realm of literary studies. However, she continues, the attitude of publishers toward Cuban-American literature has "changed for the positive." Virgil Suárez echoes this view, and he notes that because of this change, some individual writers, like Cristina García, have already entered the mainstream. Achy Obejas makes an explicit connection between this literature and that of other ethnicities that have been incorporated into the American tradition. She argues that in the near future, Cuban-American literature will deal less with Cuba and more with the United States, and all that will remain of the island will be an echo: "An echo in the same way that Irish-American literature or Jewish-American literature is; it will have more affinity to something like that, than it will to Puerto Rican or Mexican-American literature."

In several interviews, the authors emphasized that some Cuban-American writers are producing works that do not deal directly with the island. This departure from the traditional subject matter demonstrates just how much this type of literature has been absorbed into American culture. Cristina García points to her new work in progress as an example: "My next book is partly set in Iran and El Salvador. There is one Cuban part of it, but it's maybe a third of the book, as opposed to dominating the book." Dionisio Martínez emphasizes this aspect of his poetic vision, when he maintains that he doesn't "feel any obligation to anyone or any community to write a certain way." He explains that he has lived in many places, and his work reflects that variety. Even Roberto Fernández, who tended to respond to questions in short but piercing statements, had much to say on this issue. He has no doubt that Cuban-American writing is "becoming part of American ethnic literature." Like all ethnic literature, the more time that passes since the ties to the homeland have been severed, the more the literature becomes connected to the new culture: "It has to, because the link [has been] to our parents, and the next generation's link will be to their grandparents, and so on."

It may seem ironic that a book that focuses on, and attempts to define, Cuban-American literature should observe that in order to become more widely accepted, one of that literature's key components will gradually diminish. The truth, however, is that this paradox is the most salient aspect of Cuban-American literature. The literature of the Cuban exile in the United States struggles to find a voice using a language that is both foreign and appealing, in a setting that both comforts and reminds the writer of his or her discomfort. Although the evolution of Cuban-American literature is unique, it is also similar to that of literature produced by other ethnicities. Like them, Cuban-American literature will continue to slowly integrate itself into the American literary scene, while retaining its distinguishing cultural flavor.

Themes and Motifs

One of the goals of this book is to contribute to the establishment of a Cuban-American literary canon. Delineating the parameters of this literature, then, is of utmost importance. Often Cuban-American literature is discussed alongside its Puerto Rican and Chicano counterparts. This homogeneous type of grouping has led to the publication of several anthologies of Latino literature, as well as books of interviews with Latino writers.[13] Although these studies are valuable, they also help solidify the view held by some readers that one Latino group's culture and literature is indistinguishable from another's. This view is somewhat understandable, as it is, in fact, a difficult task to clearly define what makes Cuban-American literature distinctive. Some of the themes and motifs that are present in Cuban-American literature, such as an attention to family and a focus on cultural components like food, music, and religion, are also present, albeit in different ways, in other Latino literatures. There are two key ingredients, however, that seem to permeate Cuban-American literature: an interest in the role of memory, as well as an exploration of identity formation as it relates to exile.

Many contemporary scholars agree that memory and nostalgia are key ingredients in the Cuban-American sensibility. In addition to being a well-known poet and novelist, and thus one of the subjects of this book, Gustavo Pérez Firmat is also a respected critic of Cuban-American literature. He argues that Cuban exiles don't really arrive in the United States with only the clothes on their back, since they carry all their memories with them. Exile identity, by definition, is retrospective, he claims, and that's why Cuban exiles have attempted to recreate their homeland in Miami. "Even after more than thirty years of exile," Pérez Firmat asserts, "it sometimes seems that Little Havana exists in a time warp."[14] Eliana Rivero also posits that Cuban-American literature is mired in nostalgia, and she maintains that despite a fundamental difference between its Puerto Rican and Chicano counterparts, all three often attempt to recreate a past, idyllic world.[15] "Much in the same manner that a *xicanindio* present looks back longingly at the *aztlanense* past,"[16] and Puerto Ricans dream of their Borinquen, Rivero argues, "for some Cuban writers, the island that can be reached only in their dreams becomes a poetic motif."[17]

It seems natural that the works of these twelve writers often center around memory, since their own lives have been assaulted with a variety of memories, some distorted and some poignantly vivid, from their childhood in Cuba. When Achy Obejas, for instance, describes her escape from Cuba on a boat with her parents and about forty other people, she claims she's not sure which part of the trip she actually remembers, and which part is a "borrowed memory." Cristina García describes her early life in Cuba in a similar fashion. When she returned to Cuba, she wasn't sure what to expect, she states, since she had "these weird, distorted, borrowed memories." On the other hand, Dionisio Martínez claims that the sounds that the frogs made in the park across the street from his grandfather's store in Cuba "is an image that has never left [him]." Many of Virgil Suárez's memories are also vivid ones. For instance, he recounts how he still remembers helping his father slaughter turtles when hard times in Cuba forced his proud father to "forage" for food.

The memories that these writers share during these conversations are relevant not only to their lives but to their work as well, since the imaginative pieces they create are often spawned by a memory. Nilo Cruz, for instance, recalls how a conversation in the shoe store where his father worked served as the inspiration for his Pulitzer Prize-winning play *Anna in the Tropics*. When discussing his novel *Holy Radishes!*

Roberto Fernández, remembering fondly how his grandfather used to listen to Spanish music, explains with amusement, "That's where I got the idea for Rigoletto, the pig!" For Eduardo Machado, the idea that his memories of Cuba might be distorted served as the impetus for his return to the island: "When I wrote plays about Cuba, I was always thinking, 'Am I remembering it right?' 'Am I being totally unfair?'" More importantly, that return proved to be a catalyst for his future work, since now he has "no doubt anymore about the past or the present."

Several writers attempt to place the role of memory not only in their own work but also in the corpus as a whole. For Pablo Medina, although memory is an integral part of this literature, he emphasizes that the writer must be careful not to overindulge those memories, since "bad Cuban-American literature becomes mired in nostalgia." Ricardo Pau-Llosa echoes this view. He describes the creation of his poetry as a process in which memory plays an important role. However, those memories, and the emotions associated with them, are not at the center of the creative process but simply serve as a tool for it. Through phenomenology, Pau-Llosa argues, memories are converted into works of art, but only if the writer does not let him- or herself be "mugged" by those emotions. All twelve writers share their insights into the role memory plays in their own works, and through those insights, at least one of the components of Cuban-American literature is partially illuminated.

The second common theme in the works of these twelve writers is exile. In fact, most contemporary critics agree that this experience distinguishes Cuban-American work from other Latino writings. While attempting to redefine exile Latino literature, Marta Caminero-Santangelo summarizes the dominant critical stance regarding this issue: "Critical discussions of 'exile' Latino/a writing have focused predominantly on authors of Cuban origin," whereas literature produced by Americans of Mexican, Puerto Rican, or even Cuban descent is often referred to as ethnic writing.[18] The title of Isabel Alvarez-Borland's seminal study, *Cuban-American Literature of Exile*, emphasizes the notion that the work produced by these writers is centered on the exilic experience. The fact that six of the twelve writers interviewed in this book attracted Alvarez-Borland's critical attention affirms that exile and Cuban-American literature are essentially synonymous.[19]

For the writers themselves, the need to create a new sense of self, which exile has forced upon them and thus on the speakers and characters in their works, is paramount. Carolina Hospital claims that there is a strong connection between the search for identity and the exilic experience: "The insistence of going back to Cuba, and placing the text within the Cuban experience on the island . . . That's how [exile] is linked to the search for identity." This focus, she continues, on identity formation within exile is what makes Cuban-American literature different from Chicano or Puerto Rican literature. Exile is undoubtedly the most important element of Cuban-American literature, although each of these writers deals with that issue in a different way. Dionisio Martínez claims that exile is "the thread that runs through my life . . . runs through everything that I write." He explains, however, that he is "not talking about the political but about the psychological aspects of exile." For Dolores Prida, exile involves a sense of loss, and it is not only a loss of the physical but also of one's sense of place in the world: "I think it's about what we lost. Everybody's loss." Even Achy Obejas, who is the only one of these twelve writers who initially indicates that exile is not necessarily a component of Cuban-American literature, eventually remarks that "it's a defining aspect of Cuban-American literature in *this* generation."

Genre

One of the initial considerations in selecting the subjects for this book was the need to ensure that a wide range of genres would be represented. At first glance, three of these twelve writers are playwrights, four are poets, and five are novelists. These lines are somewhat blurred, however, since several have significant publications in a variety of literary forms. Although principally recognized as an anthologist, for instance, Carolina Hospital has published a book of poetry as well as a novel. Pablo Medina, whose novels are much acclaimed, also has assembled an impressive collection of poems. Virgil Suárez is an editor, a novelist, and a poet. Gustavo Pérez Firmat has a wide range of publications, including essays, critical studies, collections of poetry, a novel, and a memoir. The versatility of all of these authors is fitting, as the range of Cuban-American literature they produce seems to go hand in hand with the chameleon that is the Cuban exile himself.

Despite this crossover of literary forms, there are some generalizations that can be made regarding genre based on the comments of the writers themselves. The three playwrights assembled here, for instance, Dolores Prida, Eduardo Machado, and Nilo Cruz, all attribute their source of inspiration to Irene Fornes, the highly acclaimed Cuban-American director and teacher. Thus, influenced by Fornes, all three discuss their works in terms of characterization and observation. They all focus on visual elements, and from there, bring life to their characters. All three, of course, also create Cuban characters or scenes. This is where the similarities end, however. The Cuban characters of Eduardo Machado's plays are usually upper-middle-class men and women, members of highly dysfunctional families, whereas Dolores Prida's are often ordinary women, trying simply to survive in their new environment. Nilo Cruz creates a wide range of characters. In *Anna in the Tropics*, for instance, Cruz presents us with the educated *lector*, as well as with the illiterate cigar rollers to whom he reads.

It is a bit easier to make connections between the poets interviewed for this book. The two writers who are strictly poets, Ricardo Pau-Llosa and Dionisio Martínez, both have a penchant for moving beyond the image. Both men might begin to formulate a poem *based* on an image, or the memory of one, but, ultimately, the work that is produced has moved far beyond it. For Pau-Llosa, phenomenology is the philosophical apparatus that allows him to use his imagination to reconstitute a cup of Cuban coffee into a work of art that has little, if anything, to do with the cup itself. Dionisio Martínez might also begin with the cup, but it is simply the trigger that creates an almost endless series of related images that eventually turn into a poem. Indeed, both writers refer to poetry not as a product but as a process, a process of the imagination. This process of reimagining is aptly suited for two Cuban exiles who continuously reconstitute themselves.

The novels of Achy Obejas, Cristina García, Pablo Medina, and Roberto Fernández are as distinctive as the writers themselves: one of García's novels focuses on the Chinese presence in Cuban culture; Obejas has recently turned her attention to the Jewish past and present of Cuba's identity; Medina's last novel explores the cigar rollers of Ybor city; and Fernández holds up a mirror to the center of Miami's exile community, a mirror reflecting back a distorted image.

What are we to make of this hodgepodge of topics? The only answer that is valid is one that García herself provided during her interview: "Identity is continually evolving. It's not something fixed, and it's not 1957, and it's not listening to certain music. It's something that's continually changing." All of these novelists employ structures that reflect this evolution. The works often move from present to past and then to present again. Sometimes the point of view shifts continuously, as in

García's *Dreaming in Cuban*. Often the title of the work itself reflects this distortion and shift, as is true for Obejas's *Memory Mambo* or Fernández's *Raining Backwards*. Sometimes the shift occurs explicitly inside the work, as in Medina's *The Return of Felix Nogara*, or symbolically, as in his *The Marks of Birth*. Whatever the case, these transformations reflect the interest of Cuban-American novelists in the traumatic changes that have affected all of their lives.

Gender

The four women interviewed in this book, Dolores Prida, Achy Obejas, Cristina García, and Carolina Hospital, are accomplished Cuban-American writers and among the most widely read female Cuban-American writers of the late twentieth and early twenty-first centuries. They each have overcome different obstacles to achieve this status. Perhaps because of this, the female characters they create are themselves strong, independent women. Indeed, the female characters created by these writers are anything but subservient: they are the matriarchs of the household, and through them, the family's existence is maintained. In the interviews that follow, the comments of these four writers regarding the female persona shed light on their characterization and, more importantly, on the role of the woman in Cuban-American culture.

Carolina Hospital, for instance, maintains she has a strong interest in feminism, so it was important to her that in her novel *A Little Love*, the main character not assume the stereotypical role to which Latina women are usually relegated. Hospital argues that it is crucial to depict strong, self-sufficient Cuban women, since, in reality, "Cuban-American women are the daughters of very strong Cuban women," who have had to overcome the hardships of exile. It is important for Hospital that Cuban-American writers continue to fight against the media's negative portrayal of Cuban-American women: "I was really fed up with Latinas being depicted in the media as either the maid or the exotic seductress. I wanted to depict women professionals."

Much has been written about the role of women in the novels of Cristina García.[20] In her first book, *Dreaming in Cuban*, we are introduced to three generations of women in the del Pinos family: Celia, the grandmother; Lourdes, the mother; and Pilar, the daughter—each a tower of strength in her own way. *The Agüero Sisters* continues in this same vein, and although García's latest effort, *Monkey Hunting*, focuses on a male character, the women in his life are also powerful in their own right. García herself admits that the men in her earlier books were "more marginal." However, she explains that at least one of the women in *Monkey Hunting*, Chen Fang, remains "fairly strong," considering that "in those times, women who were exceptional got crushed." It is telling that this assertion is made in response to a question asking her to consider the connection between the fictitious Chen Fang and the real-life, modern-day Latina.

Dolores Prida has a dual advantage when it comes to discussing the role of Cuban-American women: she has not only created dozens of characters that deal with this topic, but she is also an editor for *Latina* magazine. She points out that one of the reasons her characters are appealing is the ironic conflict between the reality of the new Cuban-American woman and the stereotype that lingers in the minds of audiences. When asked about today's reaction to *Beautiful Señoritas*, for example, she jokes, "Things have changed, but they haven't changed." She argues that this is due, in part, to the repeated arrival of new waves of immigrants, who often bring with them outdated, macho views of women. Therefore, she adds, although "I work for a magazine where we flaunt our so-called sensuality . . . and it's empowering. . . . the play still works because it's still funny. I think there's still a stereotype."

The writer who perhaps best shatters these stereotypes regarding the Cuban-American woman is Achy Obejas. Her sexually charged novels often deal with issues like homosexuality and AIDS. Obejas makes it clear, however, that while her characters may be gay, her novels are not. That is, she maintains that she integrates her characters' sexuality into the thematic concerns of the story, a thematic concern that folds nicely into issues of sexual confusion, as often her characters are struggling with a larger question of identity. Obejas speaks frankly about her own lesbian lifestyle, especially when she visits her homeland, and she explains that in Cuba, "You can be as queer as you want, as long as you don't talk about it." Obejas does talk about it, however, and her characters reflect the stigmatization involved in being a gay Cuban woman in today's world.

Labeling

One of the most confusing and controversial issues surrounding Latino literature, in general, and Cuban-American literature, in particular, is that of labeling. No critical consensus exists about what is to be termed a Cuban-American text, whether or not the term itself is an appropriate one, or even what we are to call those who are engaged in creating those texts. If we are to continue to legitimize Cuban-American literature, however, the question of labeling, which is necessary for canon formation, becomes imperative. The twelve writers interviewed here offer a variety of responses concerning this issue. By discussing how they view themselves as producers of Cuban-American literature, they perhaps offer some answers regarding this slippery but crucial component of their work.

Eduardo Machado has strong feelings about labeling, especially when a label is imposed upon him. Although he refers to himself simply as a playwright, he explains he used to resent it when he was described by critics as a *Cuban* playwright. This remark seems contradictory when juxtaposed with his explanation about why he decided to become the artistic director of INTAR (International Arts Relations, one of the longest running Latino theaters in the United States): "I feel very strongly about what Cubans have to say, and . . . I want to help that marketing become a universal." The confusion is clarified when Machado explains that he didn't understand why his ability as a playwright was placed second to his Cuban origin: "The critics don't say, 'Tom Stoppard has written every combination of American,' or 'Tennessee Williams has written every combination of Southerner.'" Fellow playwright Nilo Cruz has a similar view on the subject. "I just like to see myself as a writer; period," he proclaims. However, he makes it clear that he writes about what he knows, and "what I know most about is my Cuban heritage, my Cuban culture."

Many of the other writers in this book are also disdainful of labels, but they are more willing to describe themselves as writers who produce Cuban-American literature. Pablo Medina, for example, calls himself a "Cuban-born writer" because he "doesn't want to leave that part of him behind." However, he feels the term "Cuban-American" is redundant because "all Cubans are Americans" in a hemispheric sense, and because "to be Cuban culturally is to embrace whatever historic connections there have been between the United States and Cuba." Roberto Fernández, on the other hand, has no qualms about labeling himself as Cuban-American, although not for political or cultural reasons, but for a practical one: "Well, I've written about the Cuban-American experience, so I guess that's what I am, Cuban-American." For Virgil Suárez, labeling himself a Cuban-American writer is more than nationalistic pride, it is also a way to ensure his place within literary history: "I think [that] at the end of the day, I don't mind being called a Cuban-American because . . . it's sort of a way to become immortal, in that eventually, whether somebody thinks I'm great or I'm terrible, they will at least put me in a footnote somewhere. And I really like that."

As if to underscore this divergence of opinions, the two writers who are the most diametrically opposed politically, Achy Obejas and Gustavo Pérez Firmat, agree with each other concerning this question. They both appreciate that, regardless of what they may want to be, or how others may perceive them, they are both undeniably Cuban. Obejas points out that "the fact I was born in Havana colors everything in my life." This basic fact makes any label that is used to identify her irrelevant, since, she claims, "the Cuban part of it is fixed, whether I'm a Cuban writer, a Cuban-American writer, or a Cuban who writes." Pérez Firmat has written extensively on the Cuban condition in exile, and elsewhere, he has affirmed many times that he is Cuban first. In this interview, he reaffirms that stance, by explaining that even though America may be part of his psyche, since he has lived here all his adult life, "it's not the most important part." "No matter how assimilated I may act or look," he concludes, "there is always an unassimilable remainder, a Cuban core, which only seems to get larger with the years."

Clearly, there is no definitively appropriate label to use when referring to the group of exiles assembled here. These writers' wide divergence of opinion demonstrates the uniqueness of their individual talents, once more indicating they have moved "beyond the hyphen." However, despite having lived in the United States for most of their lives, all these authors choose to integrate the Cuban homeland into much of their work, thus reflecting their view of themselves as Cuban-American writers. Perhaps Carolina Hospital puts it best when attempting to define Cuban-American literature itself: "To me, [it] is a literature that reaches out to two cultures; it's more than being Cuban or American. It's both."

Language

Almost twenty years ago, Carolina Hospital edited a collection of works by Cuban-American writers, which she subtitled *Los Atrevidos*. These writers were considered daring because they chose to write in English. Today, many Cuban-American writers are using English as their primary language, including the twelve interviewed in this book. This emphasis on the English language does not mean, however, that they have left their ancestral tongue behind. In fact, much of the work they produce serves as a vehicle for the examination of that duality they continue to feel about the role language plays in their lives. This duality is one which many of the writers discuss in the conversations that follow, and which they often trace to their first encounter with these strange and fascinating words.

Dionisio Martínez's initiation into English left a sour taste in his mouth. He recalls being lost on his way home from school and attempting to communicate with someone who might give him directions, an attempt which failed. Later, he had an epiphany after exchanging a few words with another boy: "I could actually understand this new language!" Nilo Cruz also felt lost when arriving in Miami and encountering English for the first time. He explains that this is why he forced himself to learn English quickly, because "even at that early age, I knew that as soon as I learned the language, the better it was going to be." For Eduardo Machado, acquiring the new language was a more pleasant experience, since a teacher who believed in him smoothed the way. "I took his Shakespeare class," he recalls, "and I think I got all my intellectual ideas in English." The connection between acquiring the language and developing as a writer is one Ricardo Pau-Llosa also makes. He maintains that he writes in English because he was raised in the United States, but more importantly, the "training of my imagination was in English."

Two of the writers interviewed here, who also appeared in Hospital's collection, still describe their sense of duality regarding the English language, even though they use it as a primary tool in their work. In his usual wry manner, Fernández remarks that now he writes some things in Spanish "because so many more Cuban writers are writing in English that maybe now it's daring to write in Spanish." He argues that Cuban-American literature is a reflection of the ability of these writers to transform language: "We're like chameleons. We can switch cultures. We can switch languages." Medina continues to write primarily in English, but he also publishes work in his native tongue. He explains that the duality that he feels about language reveals his poetic sensibility since his subconscious mind dictates whether the work is written in English or Spanish: "If a piece of writing comes out, say, in Spanish, well, the fact that you thought it in Spanish, that you wrote it in Spanish, whether a page or two or twenty, is telling you something about where it came from inside you. If it comes in English, then it's the same."

Most of the writers point to English as a device they use to reveal that English is only one of their linguistic weapons. The sense of word-play that this duality creates allows the writers to explore their own sense of loss by employing the language that underscores it. Virgil Suárez explains that he likes playing games, "So the fact that in English you can write the same image five different times in different ways appeals to me." "I also think," he continues, "that English has served as a filter between my memories of Cuba and my life here. It's sort of a bridge, but it's a long bridge that I have to take every day."

Without a doubt, Gustavo Pérez Firmat is the writer who best verbalizes and embodies the confusion and delight that working in two languages provides. Pérez Firmat's poetry and prose is replete with pun, paradox, and oxymoron. His penchant for linguistic play is evident in his conversation recorded here, as he cannot help using humor to explore even the most serious of issues. He explains that English is the appropriate language for such play, since Spanish has no homophones and no homographs. He also provides a personal reason for his linguistic quirks: "Perhaps I feel freer to fool around in, and with, English because it's not my mother or father's tongue." He has argued elsewhere, and he repeats it here, that Cuban-American literature is written in English. He adds, however, that Cuban-American literature "is full of English-language love songs to Spanish, love songs that happen also to be valedictories." But what accentuates this linguistic duality, he argues, is "an exile literature written in English that pines for the homeland in a language that makes that homeland more distant."

The Island

The conversations in this book reveal the versatility of Cuban-American literature, again underscoring this literature's movement beyond the hyphen. The twelve authors gathered here work in a variety of genres, write using a wide range of styles, have divergent beliefs about the role language plays in their work, label themselves differently from each other, and explore sexuality in various ways. What unites them, however, is the place they were all forced to leave behind. Although they may have divergent attitudes about their homeland, and although those attitudes may be mirrored in their work in a multitude of forms, the indisputable fact that they are all from the same island bonds them in an overarching way.

One of the myths regarding Cuban-Americans is that they all share the same attitude regarding U.S.–Cuba relations. William Luis makes this same point when he discusses the *Areíto* movement of the 1960s and 1970s in the United States, which was begun by a group of Cuban exiles who founded a magazine of the same name and who favored a more relaxed stance toward Cuba. Luis emphasizes that while most Cuban-Americans support the U.S. embargo of Cuba, not all of them "think alike."[21] Certainly, the twelve authors assembled here support that analysis.

Dolores Prida, for instance, took part in two of the early "Dialogues" in the 1970s between Fidel and Cuban exiles.[22] The articles she subsequently wrote led to her receiving several death threats. She defends her position to this day, however, as she claims that normalizing relations with Cuba is imperative since nothing else has worked. On the other side of the political spectrum is Ricardo Pau-Llosa. Pau-Llosa isn't shy about making his position known, as he condemns those who don't condemn the Cuban communist system. In fact, he feels that setting the record straight about the Cuban regime is his "existential obligation."

The political views of the other ten authors all fall somewhere between these two extreme stances, which further emphasizes the diversity within this seemingly homogeneous group. All twelve make it clear, however, that they are artists first, and their work has no political agenda.

Several of these writers have felt compelled to return to their homeland and confront whatever memories they had of the island. Achy Obejas, for instance, has traveled there frequently and has re-established a bond with Cuba. Cristina García has also returned, and she remarks that although she wasn't sure what to expect, she "was pleasantly surprised and pleased" at what she found. Just as it was for Obejas, García's return to the island partially served as a way to better understand herself and her relatives who had stayed behind: "It helped me understand the choices they made, and why they were so radically different than my father's side of the family." Pablo Medina describes his return in his *Exiled Memories*, and during the interview, he recalls the ordeal he underwent at the Havana airport. Rather than providing a sense of cohesion, it was "a very difficult, complicated, anxiety-laden trip." Eduardo Machado's fear of returning to Cuba was not a physical but a literary one: "I was terrified when I went back to Cuba that I might find I had gotten it all wrong." His return involved more than reliving his childhood, he proclaims, it was also a metaphorical step into his own work.

Although not all twelve authors have literally returned to their island, the bond they share inevitably and forcefully makes its appearance in their work and in their words. Gustavo Pérez Firmat, for example, has never been back to Cuba, and he is not sure if he ever will. When his father was alive, they talked about returning once Castro was gone, but now Pérez Firmat wonders if he'll ever go back: "What's the point of returning if [my father] can't accompany me?" Virgil Suárez's work is replete with images of Cuba, although he also has never returned. He is convinced, however, that all Cuban exiles will be able to return at some point, but that the return will create an eerie sensation: "We will reenter Cuba and start living the life of our parents or our grandparents. And in that way, we're sort of ghosts in our own lives."

Whether or not these authors have returned, or ever will return, to their birthplace is not truly what defines them as Cuban-American writers. What does is the fact that they were born there, and Cuba will always be a part of them. Their literature reflects this connection to that long-lost home. The characters and speakers these writers create express a variety of feelings about the island: some of them long for it, others feel a disconnection, and yet others remember it through the distorted lens of nostalgia. These authors' collective tie to the royal palm and the solitary star—symbols of their homeland—serves as a reminder that this literature has moved beyond the hyphen, to form the base of a Cuban-American literary canon that is, paradoxically, rich with diversity.

Nilo Cruz

photograph by Jennifer Reilley

❖ ❖ ❖

Pulitzer Prize–winning playwright Nilo Cruz arrived in the United States in 1970 at the age of nine. His early life in Cuba was particularly difficult. When Cruz was only two years old, his father was arrested for attempting to leave the country illegally and imprisoned for two years. After his father's release, Cruz recalls having to live a double life, pretending to support Castro's regime as his family made plans to escape to Miami.

While attending Florida schools, Cruz forced himself to learn his adopted language quickly. His literary sensibility translated exceptionally well, as Cruz's plays are written in a prose that is often poetic. His uncanny ability to accurately reproduce the cadence in which Cubans speak makes his characters come to life. Anna in the Tropics, *the play which garnered him the prestigious award, is perhaps the best example of Cruz's style, as it focuses on the sounds of words themselves. Set in 1929, it depicts the lives of cigar-factory workers in Ybor City, Florida. As they roll the cigars, a* lector, *or reader, recites passages from Tolstoy's* Anna Karenina. *The lives of the play's characters soon become entwined with those of the novel.*

Perhaps because his own life was suddenly changed as a result of exile, one of the motifs in Cruz's plays is exploring how characters deal with life-altering transformations. In Anna in the Tropics, *the entire tobacco industry is undergoing a drastic alteration, which the owners of the factory, Ofelia and Santiago, are resisting. Change is inevitable, however, as Cruz himself knows, and he makes that clear through the character of Cheché, who actually welcomes change.*

This type of opposition does not imply that Cruz's characters are one-dimensional. Quite the contrary is true. In Two Sisters and a Piano, *for instance, Cruz presents the reader with a Cuban military officer who is torn between his loyalty to the state and the love of a woman. Ultimately, Cruz's plays examine the power of the imagination to transform reality, whether it be for two kids in a war-torn country, as is the case in* Night Train to Bolina, *or a triangle of lovers in* Beauty of the Father.

As we walk toward the New Dramatists Center in New York City, where our conversation will take place, Cruz stops to chat with several people. He is somewhat of a celebrity in the neighborhood, yet he does not seem fazed by his status. His almost casual indifference to the fact that he is recognized is a reflection of his self-identification as an artist rather than as a voice for the Latino community. As we speak, it becomes evident that his focus is on his works' integrity, not their political impact. Cruz emphasizes his conscious choice at an early age to live the life of an artist, and he explains this decision in a calm, almost hypnotic tone, which is reminiscent of the lyrical style in which he writes.

During this conversation on June 6, 2005, Cruz discusses such issues as exile, his father's influence, homosexuality, and his most recent work, Beauty of the Father.

Works

Beauty of the Father (2004)

Lorca in a Green Dress (2003)

A Very Old Man with Enormous Wings (2002)

Anna in the Tropics (2002)

Ay, Carmela! (2001)

Hortensia and the Museum of Dreams (2001)

A Bicycle Country (1999)

Two Sisters and a Piano (1998)

A Park in Our House (1995)

Night Train to Bolina (1994)

⋅⋰⋅

EDR: You left Cuba when you were nine years old, in 1970. Can you describe that experience?

NC: It was very hard for a child, especially when you're nine years old, to have to leave your country. We had to live in a sort of duality before we left Cuba, because we had to pretend in our home that we were Communists, and that we were in favor of the regime. I would hear my family talking about plans to leave the country. I remember my mother telling me, "What you hear, you don't repeat to anyone." So, it's hard for a child to live in that kind of reality. Then, of course, coming to the United States and being faced with a new language was difficult. Being faced with a new neighborhood. There was a certain kind of fear that I think was prevalent at around that time in Miami, during the '70s, because there were a lot of racial tensions. We had certainly not experienced that in Cuba. My parents lived in a kind of fear, and they became very protective of me. So I lived a very isolated life in Miami. This was not a bad thing, because it helped inform my life as a writer. Because I sort of got used to living a solitary life, which is pretty much the life a writer lives.

EDR: I know you returned to Cuba in 1979. What was that like?

NC: That was one of the first times that they allowed families to return to Cuba and visit their relatives. My two sisters had stayed behind and gotten married and had families. My mother and I went back to visit them. So the trip had nothing to do with nostalgia, or anything of the sort.

EDR: I know your father was in prison in Cuba for a while. That must have been difficult for the whole family.

NC: Yes. When he returned home, he was basically a marked man. Our family was seen in a different light. Even though we pretended to be with the system, some people, like the neighborhood committee, knew. Our neighbors weren't as kind to us as they had been in the past. We were betraying the system.

EDR: You mentioned earlier that in Miami you were faced with a new language. How did that new language eventually become a vehicle for your work?

NC: Even at that early age I knew that as soon as I learned the language, the better it was going to be for me. So I really forced myself to speak to my teachers in English. That's how I was able to get out of the ESL [English as a Second Language] class. I felt if I could get out of that class, then I could communicate more with North American kids, and my vocabulary would benefit from that kind of dialogue. I went out of my way to advance myself and end up in those other classrooms.

EDR: Do you see the English language as an integral part, perhaps even an exclusive part, of Cuban-American literature?

NC: Let me speak to that in my own work. My first language is the Spanish language. I think and I dream in Spanish. My thought process, the way I construct it, has very much of a Spanish sensibility. The way a Spanish person would speak. That's something I try to capture in my language as a playwright. Sometimes it doesn't make much sense in the English language, and I have to construct the sentence in a different way. It's something that I'm very aware of as a writer. I'm very interested in capturing the cadence of Cuban people when they speak, but in English. I think the language itself doesn't necessarily matter. What I'm talking about is a certain kind of sensibility that I try to capture in my characters. That sensibility contains the Cuban culture.

EDR: Let's talk about language as it applies specifically to *Anna in the Tropics*. The relationship between the *lector*[1] and the cigar-factory workers is more than just about the words on a page, it's about listening to the *sounds* of the words. Can you speak to this?

NC: My plays are all very lyrical. I think that has to do with the literature coming out of Cuba, which was very lyrical. Very poetic. It's the literature that I grew up with. Reading José Martí.[2] Reading Virgilio Piñera.[3] Reading Reinaldo Arenas.[4] *Anna in the Tropics* allowed me to deal specifically with this idea of cadence. Here is a group of people who, basically, listened to stories and to literature throughout the day. Not only to newspaper articles, but novels, poetry, and plays. And I find that the literature is informing who they are, and the literature is influencing their lives. It's influencing the way they speak, and the way they behave. It just opened me up to endless possibilities, in terms of what I could do with language. It was justified that these characters could be poetic, because the whole day they were surrounded by literature. When I'm writing for the stage, I'm interested in creating a very specific reality that has nothing to do with real life per se. I take from reality. I take from the sensibility of Cuban-Americans in exile in the 1920s. But then I run to other extremes. I don't like to limit myself.

EDR: Where did you get the idea to write about the *lectores*?

NC: It was my father. In Miami, my father worked in a shoe store. I loved going to the shoe store because a lot of my father's friends would be there and converse. I remembered one of the conversations when someone mentioned the role of a *lector* in the *tabacareras* [cigar factories] in Cuba, and I became very interested in it. I asked my father, and of course he explained the role of the *lector*, and I just became fascinated by it. It always stayed with me. Already at that age, I was about eleven or twelve, I was enamored with literature. So, the fact that here was someone who read literature in the workplace was fascinating to me.

EDR: One of the motifs of the play is change. The whole cigar industry is changing, and the owners of this factory, Santiago and Ofelia, are resisting that change. What was being lost for these characters and what was lost for the *tabaqueros* [cigar rollers] of Tampa during this time? Can you place this in its historical context?

NC: I was doing a lot of research at the University of Miami, and there were a lot of pamphlets dealing with these Tampa factories. When these companies became unionized, the Cubans were very resistant to the changes. They had brought the industry to Tampa. Then the North Americans were coming in, and they were the ones who were trying to incorporate the unions. The Cubans in Tampa were resisting some of those ideas. A lot of it had to do with an outlook on life, a way of life. It's something that I find is still very prevalent in Miami. When I go to Chinatown, I see the same thing. A lot of the people are holding on to their culture.

EDR: This sense of loss, of course, is part of the exilic experience. Do you feel that this is an integral part of Cuban-American literature, as opposed to other Latino groups?

NC: Well, I can only speak to my own work. But yes, in my work, it is. I also think there are other elements, though, like the music. Cuban music. The climate in Cuba. The colors. All that has had an impact on Cuban people. When I'm writing a play, I'm creating a canvas. It could be a Cuban person that's living in some town in North America, and some of that culture has been passed on to the behavior of that character. And because I know that I'm painting through the writing, that element is present in the dialogue, and in the way that person looks at life. I try to regain what was lost through the writing. I try to regain that part of me that was uprooted and brought to the States. So, yes, I think exile plays an important role in all of it.

EDR: One of these characters you create, in *Anna in the Tropics*, Cheché, actually welcomes change. How does he fit into this loss you speak of?

NC: He brings about the death of the *lector*, which is a metaphor for the death of all the *lectores*. At the beginning of the Depression, the first people that were targeted were the *lectores*. Death is a metaphor for the loss of a tradition, unfortunately.

EDR: It seems that the *lector* reawakens Conchita's sexuality and essence; what does he do for her husband?

NC: I think that the husband aspires to be what the *lector* is. But, unfortunately, there's a tie to the macho man coming from countries like Cuba, Puerto Rico, Dominican Republic, and a lot of Latin America. They somehow have a respect for the refinement and education of the *lector*, but there's a detachment as well. I think he has an admiration for the *lector*, but his background doesn't allow him to go as far as the *lector*. However, he's the character that has an arc; he's a voyeur, really. By seeing his wife having this affair, he starts changing, and seeing his wife in a new light. At the end, he becomes almost like the *lector*.

EDR: This play won the Pulitzer Prize for Drama in 2003. You're the first Latino to achieve this. Do you feel like you're representing that community in some way?

NC: In the beginning, it was a shock. I couldn't believe that I got this award. Then, little by little, I had to learn to live with this "honor." I feel like I have a responsibility to my work, more than anything. Very early on, I made a choice to be an artist. I didn't choose to work in the world of business or academia. More than anything, I'm a playwright, and I think I have a responsibility to the art form that I chose for myself. And that responsibility is to become a better playwright, and become the voice for the people that my play represents, whether I'm writing about Cuba or Latin America. But only through the art form. I don't see myself becoming a spokesman. Early on I had to make choices for myself when I got the award, because I saw how the award was pushing me in that direction. That's not who I am. I'm not a politician.

EDR: I just used the term Latino. Is that an appropriate label? Do you see yourself that way?

NC: I just like to see myself as a writer, period. I'm interested in the future in writing about North American characters. Looking at *The Other*. Exploring *The Other*. Right now, I feel like it's a necessity. I write about what I know, and I know the most about my Cuban heritage, my Cuban culture. So, I keep writing plays about my country.

EDR: In one of your other "Cuban" plays, *Two Sisters and a Piano*, perhaps the most complex character is the lieutenant. He seems, at least momentarily, genuinely in love with María. He is not a faceless, inhumane vehicle of the state, but a torn man. Is this an accurate assessment?

NC: Yes. I really wanted him to be well-rounded. I wasn't interested in just a one-sided kind of character who just sort of conforms to the politics of Cuba at that time. I wanted someone who has a certain kind of individuality. There's a certain kindness in him, a humanity in him, that I didn't see too much as a child in that type of character. But I'm sure they exist. There are two sides to every human being, and I was interested in exploring that.

EDR: The two women who are at the center of the play, María and Sofía, have everything taken from them. Is there something being said there about the marginal role of women in Cuban society?

NC: It's very much like *Bernarda Alba*, Lorca's play.[5] It's about silencing women. About silencing that kind of sensibility. If you look at Cuba, it became very male-oriented. Sports. The military. I remember as a child seeing the coastline, and then seeing the trenches, in case there was an invasion.

EDR: War plays a major role in another one of your early plays, *Night Train to Bolina*. Is that where the idea of portraying two Latin American children in a war-torn country sprang from?

NC: Perhaps because as a child, I felt misunderstood, and I had that creative fire in me. My parents didn't understand it, especially my father. It wasn't until much later, until my early twenties, that I discovered a place in theater where I could start nurturing that voice. I think that's where *Night Train to Bolina* really came from. It was also a theme that I was always interested in. The power of the imagination. The fact that these kids could transform their reality through these games that they had invented in the cemeteries. They could really rise from the horrible situation they were in.

EDR: One of the institutions that denies these children their imaginative freedom is the Catholic Church. In fact, Sister Nora tells them that what they're doing is dirty. Is there some kind of statement there?

NC: One of the things that I notice in this country, and in Latin America as well, is a fear of sensuality. Especially of homosexuality.

It was something I was interested in exploring. There's not the same opposition to violence, though. It seems hypocritical to me.

EDR: Two of your plays are inspired by Lorca, *Lorca in a Green Dress* and *Beauty of the Father*. What is Lorca's appeal for you?

NC: I think because I'm gay, I had a really hard time growing up. My father was very critical of homosexuality. It's something that I wanted to explore. One of the things that fascinated me about Lorca was that he was a man who never defined himself politically. I mean, he was a writer of the people. Yet, somehow, he is seen as a communist by the Francistas [fascists]. He was killed and then silenced. When I was in Spain a friend of mine told me, "You know, we never learned about Lorca when I was in school." So here's a man who was completely silenced. Silenced, because through the literature, he criticized the upper class in Spain; he depicted the gypsies as the soul of the country; he wrote about the influence of the Moors. And people in Spain didn't want to hear those things. The same kind of thing happened to me when *Two Sisters and a Piano* was presented here in New York. I didn't know there were so many people who were pro-Castro, here in New York. There are a lot of African-Americans, for example, here . . . who think Castro is the answer to racism, who think Castro has abolished racism. This is not a reality. My work was being misunderstood, because here there are two women, who were not extremists. They were not your typical *gusanas*.[6] So, after that kind of reaction, I started thinking more and more about Lorca.

EDR: You've talked a lot about your memories of Cuba and of your childhood. Many Cuban-American writers explore the fragmented nature of memory, particularly when applied to Cuba. What role does memory, whether personal or collective, play in your work?

NC: I go back a lot to my childhood. To those first impressions of life all around me. To the sort of innocence that I encountered. I think that memory is somehow tied up with dreams, and dreams are tied up with the subconscious, and the subconscious is the best place to encounter art. I also think that we need a certain amount of distance. So, I might begin with a memory but then go somewhere else. It's what I learned from Fornes.[7] It's what an actor has to go through. We all prepare for roles as characters. You have to do that kind of research within yourself. Writing is a state of mind. I think memory is a way of leading me again into that state of mind.

EDR: I'd like to conclude by asking you about your latest work, *Beauty of the Father*, which I mentioned earlier. Lorca may have provided the general inspiration, perhaps, but how did you get the idea for the particulars of the play?

NC: I'm still working on it, actually.[8] It's based on my observations of a trip I took to southern Spain and southern Italy. It's the hardest play I've ever written. It's only five characters, but extremely complex. The story is about a young woman who goes to visit her father in Spain after a long separation. While there, she falls in love with her father's male ex-lover. The play examines what people are willing to sacrifice in the name of love. I've never seen this kind of love triangle on stage, so I thought this would be interesting to explore. I wish I could be more specific about the nuts and bolts of the play, but my process is so subconscious that it's difficult to intellectualize or teach. I don't want to bring it too close to the surface, really.

Roberto Fernández

∴ ∴ ∴

Roberto Fernández emigrated from Cuba in 1961, when he was only eleven years old. He holds a PhD from Florida State University, where he is currently a professor in the Department of Modern Languages. Fernández is known for his satiric portrayals of Miami's Cuban exile community, which he first depicted in Spanish in his La vida es un special *(1981), and in the subsequent* La montaña rusa *(1985). He continued this theme in his first English-language novel,* Raining Backwards *(1988), which was favorably reviewed in* The New York Times Book Review, *thrusting him into the limelight.*

If you enjoy Fernández's novels because of their humor and wit, you won't be disappointed when you meet their architect. The almost amused tone in which he describes Miami's Cuban exile community is reminiscent of some of his characters' lines in Raining Backwards. *In this critically acclaimed work, Fernández ironically employs magical realism to satirize the very notion of that literary technique. In this novel, as in all his work, Fernández blurs memory with fantasy, and he suggests that it is impossible for his characters to return to a land that has never really existed. This applies to one of the novel's characters, Mirta, who uses memory as a sexual weapon. It also applies to Nelly in* Holy Radishes!, *who attempts to reach the paradisiacal, yet unattainable, Mondovi.*

As we talk over lunch in a Tallahassee restaurant, at times Fernández seems reluctant to answer some of the questions I pose. I soon realize his reticence is not due to a concern that he might offend someone, but rather it is simply part of his almost retiring nature. When discussing issues relating to Cuba and Miami, Fernández does not resort to the biting sarcasm that is evident in his novels. Rather, his approach is gentle and subdued, and perhaps because of that, his words have an immediate and powerful effect.

The incongruity between Fernández's reserved tone and the wit of his words makes me laugh out loud several times during our conversation. It is this same incongruity and linguistic confusion, brought about by the displacement from their homeland, that makes Fernández's characters come alive. It is a beautiful April afternoon in 2005, and as Fernández speaks, I am constantly reminded why, as a satirist, he reigns supreme among Cuban-American writers.

Works

En la ocho y la doce (2000)

Holy Radishes! (1995)

Raining Backwards (1988)

La montaña rusa (1985)

La vida es un special (1981)

Cuentos sin rumbos (1975)

⋅∿

EDR: In 1988, because you were writing in English, you were one of *Los Atrevidos*,[1] and yet your most recent work, *En la ocho y la doce*, is totally in Spanish. Why the shift?

RF: Well, back then it was daring to write in English, but since then, so many more Cuban writers are writing in English that maybe now it's daring to write in Spanish.

EDR: What's the relationship, then, between the English language and Cuban-American literature?

RF: Well, if you want to be read by other generations of Cuban-Americans, you need to write in English.

EDR: So how does that relate to this latest novel in Spanish?

RF: That was a commercial decision. The publisher wanted it in Spanish. In fact, there were whole chapters that were originally in English. So the final product is a Spanish version of the English original. But sometimes I do it the other way around.

EDR: Do you think that this ability to switch back and forth between languages is not just an element of Latino literature but of Cuban-American literature specifically?

RF: Yes. We're like chameleons. We can switch cultures. We can switch languages.

EDR: Your work, whatever else it may be, is terribly funny. Where does your sense of humor come from?

RF: It comes from observing people in south Florida.

EDR: Other than that, are there any writers who may have influenced you to write in that humorous vein?

RF: I like Kurt Vonnegut, and I like Cabrera Infante.[2] Infante was writing about a "real" Havana. I was creating a sort of fantastic Miami. The Miami of *Raining Backwards* is pretty fantastic. I think my work is a kind of parody of magical realism.

EDR: Can you elaborate on that?

RF: Well, I was up to my neck in *magic realism*, so I wanted to poke fun at that.

EDR: So, would you label yourself as a satirist because of that penchant of yours for making fun of Cuban-Americans' distortion of their past?

RF: Through humor you can show how a community exists in a time warp; show how what we have created here is a fantasyland. Humor is better than preaching at people. People don't like to be preached at.

EDR: Since you speak of the audience, it seems to me that in order to fully appreciate your work, the reader has to have a familiarity with specific Cuban customs and traditions. Do you feel this limits you in a way?

RF: Well, when you read Southern literature you need the "database."[3] I think you need that database to fully appreciate many things, not just my work.

EDR: Let me ask you more about how you identify yourself, not just as a writer but as a person. Cuban, Cuban-American, Latino? Are these distinctions important to you?

RF: They're not that important because . . . Well, I've written about the Cuban-American experience, so I guess that's what I am, Cuban-American.

EDR: Can you define the "Cuban-American experience"?

RF: I think Cuban-American literature has two faces, like the month of January: facing the new year, but also drawing from the old. [The literature was] looking for an anchor. And the anchor, I think, was Miami. Except Miami is becoming less of a wholly Cuban city. It's becoming more of a Latino city. So now, I may be writing about "when Miami was Cuban." The good old days [he laughs]. I hear that from friends of mine. They say, "Oh, my God, this [Miami] is full of Central American stuff! You remember when this was . . . ?" So if Miami is no longer, then the only avenue will be to completely integrate with the United States. I mean, Cuban-American literature is like Cuban-Americans, a contradiction. Our whole life is like a schizophrenia. When I came from Cuba as a child, I was in the process of being Cuban. My parents were teaching me what it means to be Cuban. Then, when you come here, you start rejecting that. You don't want to be Jesús, you want to be Jay. Then, later on, you start making a reevaluation of your life and you realize that you're still a contradiction. Your whole life you're trying to renegotiate with yourself where you belong.

EDR: You arrived when you were eleven years old, in 1961. What was Miami like then, and what was that experience like for you?

RF: Well, we were in Miami for months, and then we moved to Vero Beach. There was no sense of urgency, really. We thought we would go back to Cuba soon.

EDR: Were your suitcases still packed, like Nelly's in *Holy Radishes!*?

RF: Not mine, but my mother's [he laughs].

EDR: How about your childhood memories of Cuba? Was writing a part of your world then?

RF: No.

EDR: Speaking of the island, unlike some other Cuban-American writers, you never depict Cuba as a place, but only as a memory, or some sort of fantasyland. You've never actually returned to Cuba. Do you have any desire to do so?

RF: I'd like to see it, but it's not something I think about a lot. I mean, how about if you go there, and then you're disappointed? I don't know how I would react to Cuba. When I fly out of the country, and then return to Miami, when the plane lands, I feel that I'm home. In Miami, I feel that I belong there. If I go to Cuba, I don't know what my reaction would be.

EDR: That's interesting that you feel Miami is home since you criticize it so severely.

RF: Well, you love a place, but at some point you realize, these people are wacko. But they're *my* people.

EDR: How has the Miami Cuban community reacted to your work?

RF: I'm not sure who's reading the work. I don't think Cuban-American literature is taught at many places there.

EDR: Like many Cuban-American writers, your work often deals with the use of memory. How does memory serve as a tool for reconstructing Cuba in your work?

RF: In my work, what you have is distorted memory. All memories, through time, become distorted and enhanced. And that's what you have in *Raining Backwards*. It's based on handed-down memories. Memories that you don't know if they're real or not. "Is this memory or fantasy?"

EDR: *Raining Backwards* is the novel that thrust you into the limelight. The work is structured as a series of vignettes that are haphazardly put together. Is this style related to your use of memory?

RF: Yes, memory is like flashes. It's chaotic. And the novel's title suggests the impossibility of return, because you can never go back to a previous life, or a previous moment of life. The people in that book think they're going back to Cuba, but it's all falsehood. I mean, they're longing for a place that doesn't exist.

EDR: Did it ever?

RF: I don't think so [*he laughs*].

EDR: One of the more interesting and pivotal scenes in that book, relating to this issue of distorted memory, is the sexual encounter between Mirta and the young man.

RF: Yes. In a way she's very practical. She's going to give this kid some sort of identity. Maybe it's the pleasure of being in touch with the past. And she's going to get some sort of sexual gratification. It's a very symbiotic relationship. She has the power because she has the past, and the kid wants that. He has become an addict for memories. He's asking for more. She's running out, and then she starts lying. And then *he* has power over *her*.

EDR: Your next book, *Holy Radishes!* picks up on this notion of a distorted memory of Cuba. However, the structure is much more linear.

RF: Yes, I wanted to challenge myself and see if I could do it there.

EDR: Where did the idea of Rigoletto the pig come from?

RF: When I was a child my grandfather used to play Spanish music. That's where I got the idea. The pig is part of Nelly's fantasyland in

Mondovi. The pig is the key to her fantasy. Remember that she buys it truffles and all that. I've been to Mondovi, in Italy, and I thought it would be interesting to use this place in a Cuban context. So when memories of Cuba are exhausted, there's Mondovi.

EDR: Can you elaborate on the relationship you see between Nelly's longing for Mondovi and the Cuban-Americans' sense of loss?

RF: In a way, it's a post-exile novel. Nelly wants to forget about Cuba. She says she wishes she was born somewhere else. Nelly is forgetting Cuba. And the answer is not coming here, because once she's here, she's not happy. So she convinces Mrs. James B. to go with her to Mondovi, where you can be whatever you want to be. So, maybe the answer is not Cuba, and it's not here. The answer is someplace else.

EDR: There is an element of tragicomedy in your work, as in the ending of this novel.

RF: Yes. As you're writing, you're not thinking about it, but later, you see it as so. Nelly and Mrs. James B. are like Don Quixote and Sancho. *Holy Radishes!* is perhaps more didactic than *Raining Backwards*, then, but I like *Raining Backwards* better.

EDR: Why?

RF: I like it because it's alive. When you think of the characters, they seem like real people.

EDR: You bring back these characters in your latest effort, *En la ocho y la doce*.

RF: Yes. I brought them back because I liked them. And because they're the same people. I used the same structure as in *Raining Backwards*.

EDR: One of the most memorable chapters in [*En la ocho y la doce*] is "Los Quince." The title's story refers to the *quinceañera*, the girl's fifteenth birthday party. How does it also relate to the fruit of the same name?

RF: It's a play on words. She's gotten really fat and big, like the fruit.

EDR: How about her spinning out of control?

RF: Well, it's funny and pathetic. She's out of control, just like the whole scene is out of control.

EDR: Speaking of pathetic, in "La Cervecería," the character is so obsessed with the past that he is willing to kill for it. Do you believe some Cuban-Americans' obsession is this strong?

RF: Well, a few years ago there was in Miami a gathering of some group. I can't recall their name, The Colonos in Exile, or something like that. And the idea was to put together affidavits and testify as to what they owned in Cuba. It was a reality for them, and they argued and fought over it! So, I just took it to the next level. I mean, it's a fantasy, but if you believe, it's reality.

EDR: It's been almost twenty years since your inclusion in *Los Atrevidos*. How do you think Cuban-American literature has evolved, and where do you think it will be in another ten years? Do you see it ever being in the mainstream of American literature?

RF: I think more and more it's becoming part of American ethnic literature. It has to, because the link [has been] to our parents, and the next generation's link will be to their grandparents, and so on. We think we're special, but we're not. We're like any other group now. We think that the whole world is preoccupied with Cuba and us. But no [*he laughs*]. I think that the people who are writing now don't necessarily show that tension that I spoke of earlier between here and there or then and now. People like Ana Menéndez.[4] My next project, a novel, which is a series of letters, which I want to call *Angry Letters*, has nothing to do with Cuba. I'm included in an encyclopedia, or dictionary, of Southern writers, and I think Virgil [Suárez] is included as well [*he laughs*]. I think it's the University of Louisiana Press.[5] So, I'm a Southern writer [*he laughs*]. In Cuba, I'm in *Escrituras Cubanas del Siglo Veinte*, published by El Fondo de Cultura Económica. So, who knows where it's going? Who knows what labels mean?

EDR: Speaking of labels, how do you label yourself? An ethnic writer, Cuban writer, Cuban-American exile writer?

RF: I don't consider myself an exile. Cuban-American literature comes from the experience of exile, and it distinguishes it from other Latino literature.

EDR: But you're writing about the exile experience, and therefore writing Cuban-American literature, but still don't consider yourself an exile?

RF: I'm an exile from Miami.

Cristina García

∴ ∴ ∴

Along with Mexican-American Sandra Cisneros and Dominican Julia Alvarez, Cristina García is one of the writers credited with the boom in literature written by Latinas that began in the early 1990s. Her much-acclaimed first novel, Dreaming in Cuban, *was nominated for the National Book Award. It traces the life of three generations of women, the del Pinos, who are each a tower of strength in their own way. It concludes with the youngest of the three, Pilar, returning to the homeland in order to come to terms with the sense of displacement she has felt all her life.*

García was born in Havana in 1958 and arrived in the United States when she was only two years old. She was raised in New York and studied International Politics at Johns Hopkins University, where she received an MA in 1981. That led to a job at Time *magazine, where she worked for seven years. Her initial novel was followed by another work tracing the lives of strong Cuban women,* The Agüero Sisters. *Her next effort,* Monkey Hunting, *is an epic tale depicting the lives of several generations of a Chinese-Cuban family.*

Monkey Hunting *shifts its focus away from the female Cuban psyche and introduces us to a Chinese man, Chen Pan, a nineteenth-century immigrant to Cuba. Using the legend of the immortal Monkey King as* the central motif of the work, García explores inheritance and loss as it relates to the Cuban diaspora. The strong female characters she is known for creating have not been set completely aside, however, as García's novel also introduces us to Chen Fang. In this memorable portrayal, we see the determination of an educated woman who struggles and survives despite the culture and historical period in which she lives.

Although García lives in Los Angeles, this conversation took place in Miami on November 13, 2004, during that city's International Book Fair. The relaxed self-assurance with which she speaks is reminiscent of one of the characters in her first novel: perhaps Lourdes, Pilar's mother, who embraces her adopted home eagerly and even starts her own successful business. This seems ironic, as it is Pilar's story that more closely resembles the author's own. In this confident tone, García describes her fascination with family myth-making, the role memory plays in her work, Cuban identity, and her forthcoming book.

Works

A Handbook to Luck (2007)

Bordering Fires: The Vintage Book of Contemporary Mexican and Chicano and Chicana Literature (2006)

Monkey Hunting (2003)

Cubanísimo: The Vintage Book of Contemporary Cuban Literature (2003)

The Agüero Sisters (1997)

Dreaming in Cuban (1992)

∴

EDR: I'd like to start by asking you about your recent anthology, Cubanísimo. What made you decide to edit an anthology and arrange it by types of Cuban music?

CG: Actually, I was asked to do that by the publisher, but they didn't give me any sort of format or limitation. After immersing myself in the literature, I came up with that organization. It just sort of rose up organically from reading the works, and feeling the rhythm of the various works, and thinking it might be fun to connect it to the music, and make those sort of unlikely groupings rather than just doing a standard chronology.

EDR: What type of research did you do for the project?

CG: Many of the works I was familiar with, and many I was not. I probably spent a year reading as much as I could. And then I just made my choices based on my own preferences. I think I say that in the Introduction, that it's wholly subjective. I think any anthology is pretty subjective. I don't think of it as a canon, although I think some of the best writers are in there. For me it was pure quality, and things that resonate with me. Things that sing.

EDR: How has the anthology been received?

CG: Well. In fact, they've asked me to do another anthology of Mexican and Chicano writers, under one roof.[1]

EDR: You mean Mexican nationals?

CG: Right.

EDR: Mexicans who are writing in Spanish?

CG: Yes, but there will be a volume in English. So, works in Spanish are translated into English and also selections from the Chicano [writers are translated into Spanish].

EDR: Let's switch to your novels for a while. Your latest effort, *Monkey Hunting*, includes a powerful female character, but its focus is Chen Pan. What made you decide to have a male character as the lead this time?

CG: It was the subject matter. I was interested in exploring the Chinese part of the Cuban identity, and that is for the most part male, because most of the workers who went to Cuba were men. So, I really had no choice [*she laughs*]. If there were women, maybe I would have gone that route. It was hard, since I hadn't really done men fully before. They were more marginal in my other books. I took on a nineteenth-century Chinese man who goes to Cuba. It was kind of a tall order for me. It took me a long time before I could really understand him and feel that I could navigate him through the world convincingly.

EDR: Why did you choose to explore this part of Cuban history and culture?

CG: I think I've been getting more and more interested in multiple hyphenated identities. People like my daughter. She's part Asian; she's part Japanese. I was interested in how these identities are negotiated, and how even the lexicon used to describe what's happening is inadequate. And I also wanted to go back in time to look at the original multicultural experiment.

EDR: How did you finally feel you got to know Chen Pan?

CG: Probably the most useful thing was reading a lot of Chinese poetry in translation. I mean, I read a ton of history about colonial Cuba, about Chinese history at the time. There's not that much written about the Chinese in Cuba. Usually, there's sort of a passing mention of them in history books. Or histories of the war, you know the Ten Years War, or The War of Independence.[2] They might have a paragraph, but next to nothing in them. I really had to make it up. I found this tiny little book called *Requiem for Chinatown* at the UCLA library, which showed old pictures of Chinatown in Havana. I also came across a primary document that had been translated from the Chinese, of an imperial investigation in the 1860s and of the abuses of the Chinese in Cuba by the Chinese government. Things like that, which I just came across. But, primarily, it was the Chinese poetry that sensitized me to what this character's sensibility might be. And because he's a farmer, I made his father the failed poet, so that he can be a little bit different than his peers, and he can think a little bit differently. That's where the Chinese poetry helped.

EDR: This book seems much gloomier than your previous works, which had a more hopeful vision. Do you think that's accurate?

CG: Well, I think it's a dark book, but I don't see *Dreaming in Cuban* as hopeful. The grandmother goes into the sea and commits suicide. The Pilar character betrayed her grandmother, and Lourdes has managed to basically kidnap her nephew.

EDR: But hopeful in the sense that Pilar has come to terms with where she belongs and who she is.

CG: I think that the difference is that *Dreaming in Cuban* can be a funny book, and *Monkey Hunting* isn't that humorous. I think it's dark throughout, but I think both end equally dark [*she laughs*].

EDR: Why did you choose the legend of the Monkey King as the central motif of the book?[3]

CG: I was kind of fascinated by it because the whole point of that tale is a search for immortality, which I think, in one way or another, people seek for themselves. Whether it's through religion, or through their children, or through their art. I think, in one way or another, whether we're conscious of it every moment or not, there's a seeking of immortality. The Monkey King was someone who did everything possible to ensure his immortality, and part of what I was exploring in *Monkey Hunting* was what gets inherited, or what gets passed on, as a way of immortality. Starting with Chen Pan, and then flashing forward to his descendants, I was exploring that notion of inheritance and legacy. To me this family's story was not dissimilar to the Monkey King's quest for immortality.

EDR: The use of memory has always been an important aspect of your work. How does it fit into *Monkey Hunting*?

CG: I think I play with it a little bit in the section on Chen Fang and Mingo Chen. About what they know about Cuba, and what they've heard about Chen Pan. And all that information is pretty erroneous. They get things wrong. I'm fascinated with how family history gets passed on. How family mythology is created. How legends are made within the family. Why certain versions of things survive as opposed to others, and who's invested in these particular versions of events. I think memory is acts of selection more than anything else. It's not anything objective.

EDR: You mention Chen Fang. Is there any correlation between how you see her and Latinas?

CG: I think she was exceptional for her time. In those times, women who were exceptional got crushed, and I think that's what happened to Chen Fang. She grew up in this unusual way because she was supposed to be a boy, so she has the benefit of an education that ended up working against her when the Cultural Revolution came.[4] But internally, I think she remained fairly strong, considering what she underwent.

EDR: Is there any kind of political ideology being explored in *Monkey Hunting*?

CG: I don't really make political statements. The politics are there to the extent that my characters are obsessed with, or caught up in, political events. It's really a story about character. I see interesting parallels. For example, Vietnam being right at the foot of China, and for over a thousand years run over by China, and sort of in its shadow. These things occur to me as I'm going along. But, ultimately, it has to be in service of the story of these particular characters. I'm not trying to wedge in a political agenda at all. I distrust that, actually, and I can kind of smell it when I read it somewhere else. I don't like it. Everything I write is political, but without an agenda.

EDR: Now that you've written three novels with Cuba as a backdrop, do you see any connecting threads to them?

CG: Each one explores issues of identity.

EDR: Those identities are strong ones. Each work, in fact, depicts Cuban women who take charge of their lives. Is this something you wanted to emphasize?

CG: In *Dreaming in Cuban* I wanted to explore how the fallout of one big political event affected the members of one family, particularly the women in one family. *The Agüero Sisters* is an example of my interest in how family myth gets made. And I also wanted to focus on loss and nostalgia, without focusing on the Cuban revolution but through natural history. I think, in one way or another, these novels explore notions of identity, and hopefully, on some level, emphasize what it means to be Cuban. We're here in Miami, where very rigid ideas of what it means to be Cuban exist, and the mindset here is "you're with us, or against us." I hate that notion. It's very exclusive. It doesn't include all of us who also consider ourselves Cuban and think very differently.

EDR: Since you bring up this issue of labels, let me ask if that is what you consider yourself. Is it Cuban, or something else?

CG: Yes, Cuban. Or Latina. It depends. A New Yorker? It depends. I'm all of the above. And I sort of resent, particularly in the Miami Cuban community, which I know very well, that if you're not *x*, *y*, and *z*, you're not one of us. That's a very limited point of view.

EDR: So, if it's all-inclusive, what does it mean to be Cuban?

CG: I think it's continually evolving. Identity is continually evolving. It's not something fixed, and it's not 1957, and it's not listening to certain music. It's something that's continually changing.

EDR: Latino literature, in general, is concerned with a negotiation of identity. Do you think Cuban-American literature deals with that issue in a unique way?

CG: I think the nature of the displacement is different. A lot of it is concerned more with exile than immigration, and I think in a way they set themselves apart from other Latino groups. Anywhere you go, like to a conference, there's always bad blood against the Cubans. There's always the sense that Cubans set themselves apart, and they don't want to be considered like other Latinos.

EDR: So, you're saying that they create that separation themselves, not that they're just perceived that way.

CG: I think they participate in it.

EDR: I know that you left Cuba at an early age and that you weren't raised in a Cuban exile community. How did you maintain an interest in your culture?

CG: I didn't really, until I started writing fiction. I grew up speaking Spanish at home, with my mother, not my father. So, for me, it was kind of a split situation. I was Cuban, really, just with my mother. Or sometimes I would be Cuban when the family got together. Otherwise it had little to do with who I was growing up. Or, at least, I didn't perceive it having to do very much with who I was growing up. It wasn't until I started writing fiction at age thirty that I realized there was this whole groundswell of stuff I had interjected [myself into] and absorbed that I wasn't even aware of. I think that if I hadn't been writing fiction, it probably wouldn't have coalesced in the same way.

EDR: Before you wrote fiction, you were a journalist. How did that experience and training inform your novels?

CG: Yes. I worked for about ten years as a journalist, most of those for *Time* magazine. It was actually extremely helpful for me. Probably more than anything, it helped in developing an eye for detail, and [in] trying to tell a story concisely and clearly. And it got me in the habit of writing. It's a great job for someone who's very curious because I got to go everywhere and meet all kinds of people. It was a wonderful way to spend my twenties.

EDR: What made you switch to fiction?

CG: Quite a few things. Probably going to Cuba in 1984. Then I lived in Miami, between 1987 and 1988, and that was a sort of culture shock. And then I started reading poetry. I think it was those three things. Sort of getting the tsunami wave of the Miami experience, together with the poetry.

EDR: I know you've said that your fiction, especially *Dreaming in Cuban*, was influenced by García Marquez.[5] Are there any other writers who inspire you?

CG: The person I return to again and again is Chekhov. I go over the short stories every couple of years. I read a lot of poetry as well. Wallace Stevens was influential.[6] It's a big mix.

EDR: What draws you to Chekhov?

CG: His humanity. His humanity and his economy of language.

EDR: Let's go back to that first trip back to Cuba for a moment. What did you find?

CG: I went with my sister for a couple of weeks, and it was still very much . . . [she hesitates] . . . I didn't go back for another eleven years. So that '84 trip, there was still the sense, you know . . . [another pause] . . . the neighborhood committees were still up and running, and if you said something, you had to close the blinds. On the other hand, I think I got a bigger picture of what life was like there, and why those particular family members had decided to stay and, at that point, were still very supportive of the revolution. It helped me understand the choices they made, and why they were so radically different than my father's side of the family.

EDR: Can you expand on that a bit? The choices they made.

CG: What socialism meant to them. Not just sort of theoretically, but in a real way, and how that was significant for them. Also to explore the prejudices of the family that left, and their perceptions and misperceptions of the U.S. It sort of completed the picture for me. I was hearing [the relatives who stayed behind] being demonized my whole life, and I was very curious to meet "the enemy."

EDR: So, like in your novels, especially *Dreaming in Cuban*, was there a difference between what you expected and what you found?

CG: I had no memory of Cuba. I left when I was two years old. I had these weird, distorted, borrowed memories from my mother, in particular. So, for me, it was a particularly novel experience. I didn't really know what to expect at all. I was actually pleasantly surprised and interested.

EDR: Since *Dreaming in Cuban*, many other Cuban-American writers have found success in poetry and prose. How do you think Cuban-American literature has changed since then?

CG: Yes, there are many more voices. I was talking to Ana Menéndez not too long ago.[7] Her book is set in Turkey. It has nothing to do with Cuba. My next book is partly set in Iran and El Salvador. There is one Cuban part of it, but it's maybe a third of the book, as opposed to dominating the book. I think ultimately you come into your own, where you have the freedom to write about anything that interests you, as opposed to what you're rooted to.

EDR: Have the attitudes of presses changed in accepting work by Cuban-American authors that don't contain the expected themes and setting?

CG: I remember one publisher saying years ago, "Oh, we already have a Cuban." You wouldn't hear that today. So, I think it's changing. What I would hope is that young Cuban-American writers today would feel the freedom to write about whatever interests them. If it happens to be identity issues, or about exile, great. But if he's interested in the Middle Ages and wants to write a novel set there, then he should write it. That's real progress: Having that freedom and having all those variables at your disposal; not being secluded or isolated into your own hyphenated American-ness.

EDR: Can you say more about the novel you're working on now, which you alluded to earlier?

CG: It starts in the late '60s, and there are characters in three places.[8] Originally, I thought it was going to weave [together], and they'd end up together more, and they really don't. There's a woman in El Salvador, there's a woman in Tehran, and a Cuban who grows up in Las Vegas with a father who's a magician. At one point, all of them end up in California. It's the story of all three of them. People who come from different revolutions, variously dislocated, and from different walks of life.

EDR: So, you continued with the narrative strategy of multiple voices. Is there also a shift in time, as in the other novels?

CG: No, it's pretty much going chronologically from the '60s to the early '90s. It also touches on the issue of memory, but not in the same epic way the others do.

Carolina Hospital

∴ ∴ ∴

Carolina Hospital recently published a collection of poems titled The Child of Exile, *and a few years ago, she co-authored a novel with her husband, Carlos Medina. These recent successes, however, cannot over-shadow the accomplishment that initially thrust her into the limelight: her anthology of works by Cuban-American authors writing in English.* Los Atrevidos, *aptly named since these writers dared to defy convention, was the first collection of Cuban authors making a conscious effort to leave their ancestral language, if not their culture, behind.*

Hospital left Cuba in 1961 at the age of four. She lived in Puerto Rico for five years, and then moved to Miami where she has resided ever since. In addition to her published longer works, her individual poems and stories have appeared in various literary journals and magazines throughout the United States. She holds an MA from the University of Florida, and she teaches literature and writing at Miami Dade College.

One of her most anthologized poems, "Dear Tía," illustrates the the-matic concern of Hospital's poetry. In it, a woman attempts to connect with her Cuban aunt, but the image is distorted through the shifting lens of memory. The woman's attempt to remember her aunt is symbolic of the Cuban exile's search for identity, which is at the heart of Hospital's work. This quest for identity is what has also led Hospital to collect and publish the works of Cuban writers in Florida, to underscore that Cuban writers in Florida share a common heritage with those on the island.

We met for this interview at a small deli, close to Hospital's home in South Miami, on November 12, 2004. The displaced and insecure persona that is presented to us in The Child of Exile *bears no resemblance to the tall, confident woman sitting across from me. An educator for over twenty years, Hospital speaks passionately about the importance of teaching Latin American literature to her predominantly Latino students. As an anthologist, her insights regarding Cuban-American literature are particularly instructive. During this conversation Hospital also addresses issues of gender, language, and identity.*

Works

The Child of Exile: A Poetry Memoir (2004)

A Little Love (with Carlos Medina, 2000)

"Heading to Havana," in *Naked Came the Manatee* (1996)

A Century of Cuban Writers in Florida: Selected Prose and Poetry (1996)

Everyone Will Have to Listen: The Poetry of Tania Díaz (translator, with Pablo Medina, 1990)

Cuban American Writers: Los Atrevidos (1988)

⋰

EDR: I'd like to start by talking about your groundbreaking anthology, *Los Atrevidos*, published almost twenty years ago. How did that come about?

CH: Then, I was a student at the University of Florida. I had read a lot of North American writers as an undergraduate, but I did my graduate work in the Foreign Languages Department. During that time, I discovered Latin American writers. I decided then that I would write my master's thesis on the children of exile. I was curious about people like myself, Cuban-Americans who were the children of exile [and] who were writers. Who were they? What were they writing about? After gathering all the material for the thesis, I thought, I've put so much energy into this, why not develop my own anthology? The frustration of working without significant sources for the thesis made me realize there was a need for such a collection. Interestingly, at first some of the poets hesitated because they were afraid of being pigeonholed. These were mostly younger writers, just starting, and they really wanted to mainstream, so there was some hesitation. But I convinced them by talking about filling a void, coming together as one voice—what you can't accomplish sometimes as an individual you can do united. It was a literary presence that I was looking for, together, as Cuban-American writers. I wanted to do what the Chicanos and the Nuyoricans[1] had done. I thought that this was the beginning of a new generation reflecting that bilingual existence. I wanted writers who felt that their voices were in English, while experimenting with being bicultural.

EDR: Was the daring nature of their work that they were writing primarily in English?

CH: I had taken part in a photo exhibit on the Cuban presence in Miami, and one of those images was of a restaurant with the name *Atrevidos*. It was owned by two men who had just come from Cuba and asked for a loan to open this restaurant. That triggered in my mind: What gall! Who do they think they are? Well, that's what these writers were doing. They were trying to forge new territory by being bicultural.

EDR: How do you think things have changed for these writers since the publication of that anthology?

CH: I think many of these writers have now mainstreamed. Attitudes have changed for the positive. Back then, it was different. When the anthology was first published, I went to do a reading at the Miami Book Fair. When the organizers found out it was an anthology of Cuban-American writers, they sent me to the committee that dealt with scheduling Spanish-speaking authors, and when I spoke to them, they sent me back to the committee of English-speaking writers. It was frustrating. No one knew what to do with us. I was also attacked once at a symposium because I was daring to call this Cuban literature, even though it was written in English. Things have certainly changed. People don't do that anymore.

EDR: So, you think Cuban-American literature, in general, has changed as well?

CH: Let me explain that using my own experience as a writer. One reason I stopped sending out manuscripts is because I started getting comments like, "Yeah, it's a good poem, but it's not what we're looking for. It's not cultural or political." I realized after a while what editors wanted: if you were Latina, you had to give them what they expected a Latina to be writing about. When I began to expand beyond identity issues into themes of, let's say, motherhood, or love, or especially feminism, a lot of the publishers no longer showed an interest. I think, however, the attitude, in terms of Latin women, has been altered a bit. I mean, Miami is full of Latina professionals. I'm sure it's like that in other major cities. Cuban-American women are the daughters of very strong Cuban women. In Cuba, during the Ten Years War so many men died that women had to open guesthouses and become independent, and then again with The War of Independence.[2] And once again with the whole process of exile. These women were thrust into situations where they needed to be strong, not only in character, but economically and professionally. Society had to change because of those historical events.

EDR: Do you think that writing primarily in English is no longer a requisite characteristic of Cuban-American literature?

CH: I'm very much against labels. What is Cuban-American literature? It's written by people who are both Cuban and American, and if they choose to write in Spanish, or if they choose to write in English, or if they choose to write in Spanglish, as Ilan Stavans[3] has now legitimized, who am I to say? Authors write the best literature they can, and they choose whatever is true to themselves, what's authentic. To me, Cuban-American literature is a literature that reaches out to two cultures; it's more than being Cuban or American. It's both, I suppose.

EDR: In addition to this bilingual aspect, are there other motifs that you believe are staples of Cuban-American literature?

CH: I think so. I think some of the themes are a strong emphasis on the search for identity—because of being bicultural, and bilingual, because of being displaced. The last line of my poem "Dear Tía,"[4] which reads: "I write because I cannot remember at all," strikes a chord with people. I think it's that theme of being between cultures and trying to find home, and being told that you're this, but feeling that you're more than that or less than that. I think identity is a very strong theme.

EDR: But that's an issue that is prevalent in other ethnic literature. How is it distinctive in Cuban-American literature?

CH: What makes it distinctive is the exile experience, which is different than the immigrant experience. That aspect manifests itself in the literature itself, in the insistence of going back to Cuba, and placing the text within the Cuban experience on the island. That's how it's linked to the search for identity. I don't know that many Chicano writers are setting their novels back in Mexico City or Nuyoricans back in San Juan. And yet you find writers such as Cristina García who has a novel that takes place in Havana.[5] Pablo Medina's last novel takes place almost entirely in a fictitious place that we're supposed to believe is Cuba.[6] Sandra Castillo, a young writer, has her first poetry collection about her trip back to Cuba.[7] I think maybe it has something to do with being an exile, a sense of incompleteness, or a sense that there's still something that needs to be resolved, that perhaps you don't have in an immigrant population.

EDR: How about your own arrival from Cuba? How did that help shape your consciousness as an artist?

CH: Well, I left Cuba when I was four. My father was an electrical engineer. It's like many other stories. We left in 1961, and my father had seventy-five dollars in his pocket. We went thru Jamaica and into Puerto Rico, and we stayed with friends of my father for months, maybe even a year, all five of us in one room. He was able to rebuild his career little by little. We stayed in Puerto Rico for five years. Then we came to Miami when I was nine. My father worked at Florida Power and Light, doing the equivalent of what he did in Cuba. I went to Catholic school, and then started college here.

EDR: You didn't speak English, I suppose, when you first arrived?

CH: No, I didn't speak a word. I remember crying a lot. I cried every day for about six months. It was a really quick immersion. There was no bilingual program. I just learned English. I became a real Americana. And then I got to the University of Florida in Gainesville, and everyone kept saying, "You're so Cuban; you're so Cuban." And I thought to myself, "What are you talking about? I'm this gringa hippie." But then I decided, if everyone is so sure I'm Cuban, I'd better know what being Cuban means. That's when I began to research what it meant to be Cuban. I took courses in Cuban history. I switched from an English degree to Latin American literature. That was a great education for me. I was able to meet many Cuban writers invited to the university. Very soon after they arrived from Cuba, I met Heberto Padilla, Reinaldo Arenas, Roberto Valero.[8] Really powerful experiences that opened my eyes. When I met Roberto Valero and Reinaldo Arenas, for example, I realized [that] to them, living on an island was like being trapped in a cage, and the ocean was what separated them from freedom. It was a dramatic loss of innocence for me to understand this perspective from writers I was meeting in the flesh. I had an illusion of an island, [which] was shattered. I think that's when I began to forge more of a complex cultural identity, and what led me to my own creative writing. I started anthologizing, but eventually, I let go of that, because what I really wanted to do was my own creative work.

EDR: Despite that, you published another anthology in 1996 which placed Cuban authors in Florida in their historical context.

CH: It seems recent, but it really isn't because it took about six years to put together. That anthology came about through suggestions from different people, especially Ricardo [Pau-Llosa], who encouraged me. He said, "What you did in *Los Atrevidos*, why not expand it and place these writers in their historical context?" I thought about it and agreed. It became a very personal project for me. Part of the problem of being a child of exile is that sense of, "Where are your roots?" or "Where are you going?" The book helped me explore the history of Cubans in Florida and made me see that it's not so different from that of Cubans in Cuba. For example, I found out that when the British took over Florida, many of the Cubans here returned to Cuba; therefore, some of our ancestors are original Floridians. I thought, why not write an anthology that connected us more than separated us? I wanted to show that we're not just some random people who showed up here one day. The connection goes back centuries. I wanted to show that we're not just an anecdote. The link between Cuba and Florida is strong.

EDR: Recently, you finally did focus on your own creative work. Let's talk about your novel *A Little Love*. How difficult was it to collaborate on that with your husband and maintain a solid marriage?

CH: Let me tell you how that came about. My husband [Carlos Medina] was always very supportive of my work. Before this novel, I was asked to collaborate on *Naked Came the Manatee*, which became a *New York Times* bestseller. My husband helped me with that; we did it together, and it was so much fun. Then one day, I was at a poetry reading, and a woman approached my husband while I read and asked if he knew anyone who was doing fiction, a contemporary novel. He told her to talk to me, and when she did, I told her that most Cuban-American works were dealing with issues of nostalgia or identity, but there really wasn't anything that was modern and jazzy, dealing with Miami from a Cuban perspective. Walking home that night, my husband and I decided we would give it a shot, together. Later it turned out, by the way, that the woman became our agent for the project. We thought about how many Cuban writers didn't live in Miami. Yet, here we were, he and I, both writers living in Miami. One of my interests was pursuing something innovative. The novel's not about Cuba. It doesn't mean that the characters don't have an interest in Cuba, but their lives are primarily here. The story's about looking forward, not looking back. I can't write about Cuba. I don't have an interest in writing about Cuba. I left Cuba when I was four. Why should I write that story? My other interest is feminism, and I was really fed up with Latinas being depicted in the media as either the maid or the exotic seductress. I wanted to depict women professionals. I think it was also important for me to validate the experience of Miami.

EDR: Can you explain that?

CH: I think outside of Miami, there's a real misconception about the city. When I travel and I tell people I'm from Miami, I get all kinds of bizarre reactions. There's this idea of a homogeneous Cuban entity; people generally don't understand the subtleties and complexities of Miami. The variety and diversity within it, even within the Cuban-American community. There are generational differences, political differences, cultural differences, class differences, and community differences.

EDR: In addition to this prose work, you also published a collection of your poetry called *The Child of Exile*. You had published many poems individually, and some have been anthologized frequently. Why did it take so long to put them all together in a collection?

CH: When I was young, I started publishing individual poems. Then there came a point when I started to send out manuscripts, and it was very difficult and time-consuming. So I decided I needed to spend the time writing instead. I got tired of waiting to hear from publishers. I was doing other things that were fulfilling and fun. Once the novel came out, actually right before that, I was diagnosed with breast cancer. The last poem in the poetry collection, which is a poem of thanks, closes a chapter in my life. That influenced my decision to send out a new poetry manuscript. I had finished the novel and had collaborated on several projects. The poetry was all mine, something I had to do on my own. I decided it was time to take the best of what I had written in the last twenty years and put it together.

EDR: What are you working on now?

CH: I'm working on poems. I have a series on the theme of the working mom. I also have other fiction projects. My teaching keeps me busy, too. The writing process is very important to me because that's mainly what I teach. I teach composition and creative writing. And when I teach World Literature, I teach some of the Latin American writers I love, because of the population here. Being a writer myself allows me to reach my students at a deeper level.

Eduardo Machado

❖ ❖ ❖

Eduardo Machado was born in Havana and came to the United States when he was eight years old. He grew up in Los Angeles and now lives and works in New York City. In addition to directing Columbia University's graduate playwriting program, he is also the artistic director of INTAR, one of the country's first Latino theaters. He is a prolific writer who has authored over forty plays, many of which have been produced at major regional theaters, as well as in Europe and off Broadway.

He has received numerous awards, including the Berrilla Kerr Grant (2001), for his contributions to American theater, a National Endowment for the Arts Fellowship (1999), a Dramalogue Award for Best Play (1991), a Ford Foundation Grant (1993), a Rockefeller Foundation Playwriting Award (1985), a National Endowment for the Arts Playwriting Grant (1981), and a National Endowment for the Humanities Youth Grant (1978).

Machado's plays might be described as containing a Victorian sensibility. His characters, mostly upper-middle class and well educated, usually project an appearance of self-assurance and propriety. Behind this facade, however, their lives are tumultuous. Infidelity, incest, and homosexuality are but a few of the topics that lie beneath the surface of his seemingly pristine scenes. This is exactly the case in Fabiola, *where the pursuit of material possessions is paramount in the characters' lives. This obsession with consumerism, along with a self-indulgent hypocrisy, leads to an almost amoral existence. The discrepancy between the facade and the reality is also readily apparent in both* Havana Is Waiting *and* The Cook. *In both these plays, the stark differences, as well as the affinities, between Cuban exiles and those who stayed behind illustrate the complexity of the Cuban equation.*

When I meet Machado, I am struck by this same sense of formality. His own upper-middle-class upbringing is apparent in his polite and somewhat reserved mannerisms and speech patterns. The incongruity between Machado's sense of decorum and the chaotic and frenzied pace at the INTAR offices in New York City, where we meet, is dramatic.

During our conversation Machado describes his return to the homeland, his creative process, and his feelings about living and working in exile. The date is July 20, 2004.

Works

Tastes Like Cuba: An Exile's Hunger for Home (2007)

Cuba Libre (2007)

A Pure Stranger (2007)

Paula (2006)

The Poet Matador (2005)

Kissing Fidel (2005)

My Sister (2004)

The Conductor (2004)

Secret Tapes (2004)

In Old Havana (2004)

That Tuesday (2003)

The Cook (2003)

The Flag (2001)

Havana Is Waiting (formerly, *When the Sea Drowns in Sand*) (2001)

Crocodile Eyes (1998)

Cuba and the Night (1998)

Between the Sheets (1997)

Closet Games (1995)

Three Ways to Go Blind (1995)

Breathing It In (1995)

How I Found My Way Back to Rosario (1993)

When It's Cocktail Time in Cuba (1991)

In the Eye of the Hurricane (1991)

The Floating Island Plays (1991)

Stevie Wants to Play the Blues (1990)

Related Retreats (1990)

Fiancés (1989)

A Burning Beach (1988)

Don Juan in New York City (1988)

Wish You Were Here (1987)

Why to Refuse (1987)

When It's Over (1987)

Once Removed (1987)

Fabiola (1986)

The Perfect Light (1985)

Finding Your Way (1985)

Broken Eggs (1984)

The Modern Ladies of Guanabacoa (1983)

Rosario and the Gypsies (1982)

They Still Mambo in the Streets of Rio (1982)

See Emma Run (1982)

Embroidering (1981)

·:~

EDR: I want to start with a difficult topic, the Peter Pan exodus.[1] I understand you were one of those children?

EM: Well, I want to clear that up. I came under that visa, but I stayed with my uncle and his wife for a year. So I had it much better than most kids who came under the Peter Pan visa. I came with my brother who was four, and I was eight years old.

EDR: So you must remember quite a bit about your early childhood in Cuba.

EM: Yes. I grew up in Cohima, which is a town about twenty minutes from Havana. One of my grandfathers owned a bus company, and my other grandfather was the second-in-command of the docks in Havana. It was the typical upper-middle-class childhood in Havana.

EDR: Anything in particular from those early years that stands out?

EM: I used to have more memories until I went back to Cuba. Since then, it's changed because I remember Cuba as it is now. But yeah, I had a lot of memories of my childhood that turned out to be accurate. I found my way home in a car when I went back, even though they've renamed the streets. So now that I've been back, I think that I had a pretty accurate memory of where I lived. I found my way back to my school, which was in Guanabacoa.[2]

EDR: How was your work affected by those memories?

EM: I was terrified when I went back to Cuba that I might find I had gotten it all wrong. I was in a state, half because I was going back to Cuba, and half because I'd thought I had gotten it all wrong. When I went back, especially to my hometown, I was terrified because not only was I walking into my childhood but also walking into my fiction. That was a very profound and overwhelmingly painful experience. The two things mixed while I was there. The reality of the place and the reality of the reality came together, and it was very life-changing in many ways for me.

EDR: This was in 1999.

EM: Yes, and I've been back many times since then. I just went again about a month ago. When I go back there now, the past is gone. The past that's there now is the past that I've created there since 1999, and the past of 1959 is gone.

EDR: Is that a good thing?

EM: I think it's a great thing. I think it's been a great thing for my writing because my writing needed to go somewhere else. I think I went back for my writing, because I felt that I had gotten as far as I could get without going back.

EDR: Can you explain that?

EM: I have no doubt anymore about the past or the present, so I don't feel insecure about what I have to say about it. Before, when I wrote plays about Cuba, I was always thinking, "Am I remembering it right? Am I being totally unfair?"

EDR: Why is that important to you as a creator of fiction?

EM: Well, when I first started writing, I didn't care much about it. But when my plays actually started being produced, and I realized that what you write is going to be used both culturally and politically to represent a group of people (because if you're a minority, that's what happens), then I started thinking about it. Both the people living here and the people in Cuba use the work as a political tool. So I became aware, right from the first play that was produced, that that's how it was being perceived. Therefore, the work was no longer just personal. So I worried about it a lot. I really did. And now I don't, because I feel I've done enough detective work to know how both sides feel. Therefore, I can have my own opinion about how I feel without feeling guilty.

EDR: Since you bring up this issue of representing a group of people, how do you feel about labels? How do you label yourself?

EM: I describe myself as a playwright, and I train playwrights of all nationalities. I am described by others as a *Cuban* playwright.

EDR: And how do you feel about that?

EM: It's fine with me now. I used to really resent it. I got to be just a playwright only once when I wrote a play called *Stevie Wants to Play the Blues*, which was not about Cubans, and then nobody mentioned the fact that I was Cuban. They just mentioned the fact that I was the playwright. That was liberating. That was very liberating. But you have to learn how to use the marketing media. I've decided to become the artistic director of a Latino theater for a reason. I feel very strongly about what Cubans have to say, and I want to help that marketing become a universal. For example, there was a review in *Variety*, which was a positive review of my last play, but it really pissed me off. I usually don't get mad at reviews, but this one really pissed me off because it said, "Mr. Machado has written about every combination of Cuban you can think of; apparently he thinks there's more to say." The critics don't say, "Tom Stoppard has written every combination of American," or "Tennessee Williams has written every combination of Southerner." It's so racist at its core, and I'm sure the person didn't even think they were being racist. I'm sure the person thought they were giving me a compliment.

EDR: You were being pigeonholed as a creator of Cuban-American literature, and not just a playwright.

EM: Exactly.

EDR: If there is such a thing as strictly Cuban-American literature, what would you say are its characteristics?

EM: Well, I think it's a matter of nationality. By definition, I think I write Cuban-American literature because I'm Cuban, even if the topic is not Cuba.

EDR: Well, let's restrict it to Cuban-American theater. What would you say that's about?

EM: I think it's less about eccentricities. It's about who we are as a people.

EDR: Which is?

EM: Nomads with a home. We're still nomads because we still want to go back. That's the common theme. And when you go back, you know why. Because it's unbelievably beautiful and intellectual and alive. Once you go back, you have no doubt why. It must have been an impossible place to run away from. That must have been tragic. It must have been earth-shattering. When you see the city, and you see the life that they left.

EDR: Before you were a successful playwright, you were an actor, correct?

EM: Yes. When I was seventeen, I decided to become an actor, and I was in L.A. and went to acting school, and I was getting parts in sitcoms. Then I joined this group one summer, called the *Padua Hills Writers Conference*, as an actor, and I was acting there and met Maria Irene Fornes,[3] and I started writing. I came to New York to be an actor. I was a member of the Ensemble Studio Theater, as an actor. Then I got an NEA grant for my first play because I had a reading of it in the Ensemble Theater. It was $12,500, which was a lot in 1981, and all my writer friends got upset. So I decided I was going to write as many plays as I could to prove to them that I deserved this, and I stopped acting. I came here, to Irene's workshops, and started writing plays. That year I wrote

Fabiola, *Rosario and the Gypsies*, *The Modern Ladies of Guanabacoa*, and *Broken Eggs*. And then EST decided to produce *Modern Ladies* before I finished writing it, and they produced it the following year, and they produced *Rosario and the Gypsies* that summer.

EDR: Let's talk about your teaching of playwriting. I know you have a group of very successful students. What sort of techniques do you help your students follow?

EM: Well, I studied with Irene, where everything is very visual. You're seeing a scene in front of you, and you're writing down what they were doing, and what the characters were saying. When I started teaching, I thought, well, that's interesting, but I don't want to teach the same exact way Irene teaches. So I started thinking, well how do *I* write a play? Well, I was an actor, and I studied [Konstantín] Stanivslasky, and I really found the conflict inside myself and gave some to each character. So, I started developing a series of exercises that have to do with developing a character: what does a character need, and when did *you* need it, and where is it in your body, that need? Then that opens the students up to really listening, because most people when they're writing hear two voices. One's the real voice, which is a real scary one, because it might lead nowhere. The other is the linear one, which is telling you "the plot, the plot, the plot." The trick to playwriting is to get in touch with the first voice enough so that the scene has poetry and dimension. So, I have my students let their minds stop and have the imagination create.

EDR: Is that voice that you hear always in English?

EM: It's always been in English. I've tried to have it be in Spanish. I went to Cuba once for a month just to write a play, to see if I could, if I was talking Spanish all the time. I think I wrote the first two pages, and then I switched immediately to English.

EDR: So, at eight years old, when you arrived here, how difficult was it to learn English?

EM: I spoke Spanish all the time. My mother doesn't speak English. I had this wonderful English teacher in high school who really believed in me. I took his Shakespeare class, and I think I got all my intellectual ideas in English. And then, as an actor, I only acted in English. Everything I know about a play was always in English, and I think that's why I create characters in English.

EDR: Tell me more about giving your characters some of your conflicts. Your plays are not autobiographical.

EM: It doesn't have to be the story, but the yearnings of the characters. The characters and I just start talking. It's just a matter of freeing the mind and not worrying. People think that plays are what they read in books, but plays are a process of re-writing that ends up being a play, that has to start with something raw. And the raw thing scares people.

EDR: What do you mean by the "raw thing" exactly?

EM: The raw thing might not have any structure, and you might not know where it's going, and that scares people because the thought of not knowing where you're going is frightening.

EDR: You said earlier that you felt more at ease with yourself now. Does that mean that you know where you're going?

EM: I know how to write a play. And I know how to teach. Do I know how to run a theater? I don't know yet.

EDR: And do you see a connection between that knowledge and your trip to Cuba?

EM: I think I became more secure about my subject matter. It's very hard to write about this place that you were eight years old the last time you saw it. In many ways, it's like: "How dare you?"

EDR: Let's talk a bit about *The Floating Island Plays*.⁴ One of the first plays you ever wrote is in that collection, *Fabiola*. How did you create that character?

EM: My uncle was married to someone named Fabiola. She died in childbirth. He went crazy. And I grew up with that as a kid.

EDR: *Fabiola*, and the other plays in that book, often bring up the topic of capitalism. Why is that an important issue for you?

EM: I think capitalism ruined the world. And I think the pursuit of money in my family ruined their family values. The pursuit of money became more important than the pursuit of religion, self-respect, history, and right and wrong. I wrote those plays to try to figure out who they were, my relatives, and to try to figure out what they were guilty of, and why they had a revolution, and what happened.

EDR: How does the incestuous relationship in the plays fit into that?

EM: Because it's self-love. It's self-love to the point where there's no outside world. And I wanted to say: For these people, there's no outside world, and that's one of their problems. They're so vain and self-involved, and there's nothing outside of that. They're so scared of the world.

EDR: Sonia seems to be the connecting thread in these plays. Would you describe her as a strong woman?

EM: Yes, women are stronger in my earlier plays. I think that's because I like my mother better than I like my father. There are some strong male characters, though. Oscar Hernandez in *Modern Ladies* is a pretty strong character, even though he falls apart in *The Eye of the Hurricane*. In *Havana's Waiting*, there are no female characters, only men, and I think they're strong characters.

EDR: Your plays are about Cuba, but not really about what some might call the dilemma of being Cuban-American.

EM: I never felt any angst about being here. I felt the angst about not being able to go home, but I never felt nostalgic, or sentimental, about what I thought home was, because I have a very prickly family that doesn't let you feel nostalgic about things. They're very witty. As I've gotten older, I'm very glad they are who they are, because they make very interesting characters. There wasn't ever any nostalgia, though. And I grew up in L.A., so there wasn't any of that Miami stuff, and my parents weren't very interested in Cuba. *Broken Eggs* and *Once Removed* come the closest to that. *Havana's Waiting* is all about going back and facing the sentimentality and seeing what's real.

EDR: To follow that thought, it seems that exile didn't make the families in your plays dysfunctional; they were already that way.

EM: Right. They just changed locations. People need to take a responsibility about why they had a revolution. Why do you get betrayed by a leader? What were you thinking? What were you doing? And I think that sentimentality keeps you away from that, and that's dangerous, because writing is about thinking about the options. Why didn't they take them? What decisions did they make? [I'm] not blaming them, but just showing those decisions.

EDR: Can you tell me about the title of the plays, the "floating island," and its connection to the dessert of the same name.[5]

EM: That's because I thought my memory of Cuba was syrupy and fluffy, like the dessert, and because it was a little bit hard to make. And because my mother always boasted that she could make it. And it was something that was so far away. I felt if I created it for myself, I wouldn't miss it so much. I did miss it. I don't anymore. Last time I was in Cuba, I was really ready to leave, because I feel that it's stuck in [a groove of] a record that doesn't move.

EDR: The country itself is stuck?

EM: Yes. My possibility of being anything but a tourist there is stuck. So, how can I live in it? Write in it? Because it really doesn't change. I noticed that there was no movement this time. I knew a lot about it this time, and it was stuck, and I was stuck in my relating to it.

EDR: Let's talk about *The Cook*. It's set in a Havana mansion, yet it follows the life of a cook named Gladys. Why did you want to tell this story?

EM: Well, let me tell you more about the play. Gladys remains in Cuba. It starts in 1958 on New Year's Eve, and the woman of the house is leaving and tells her to please keep the house the same for her. And the cook promises to do so because she believes the lady really loves her. And the next part is the cook doing whatever she has to do so that Fidel never walks into the house. The last scene is in 1997, when the lady's daughter returns to Cuba, and Gladys is running a *paladar*.[6] I wrote this play because I went to Cuba to write about prostitutes, and when I started interviewing them, they quickly bored me. Then I noticed that there was a picture of a blond woman on the wall of this paladar I went to, and [I] found out it was a picture of the lady who used to own the house where the owner of the paladar [had] cooked. So, I went home and started writing this play. I never asked her any questions beyond that. This is the play that I'm the proudest of because I think that it manages to show the contradiction of all the sides of the Cuban equation.

EDR: Can you explain that.

EM: Because it's about Cuba from the point of view of somebody who stayed in Cuba, about the people who left. And it's written by me, someone who also left. It's also about someone who's not a Communist, who's just surviving there, and her husband who is a Communist. It's also about her cousin who gets destroyed because he's gay, and her husband's daughter and her future, and how she sees it. It has a lot of generations and a lot of different classes of Cubans within a five-character play. And it poses the question, the real question for me, which is how do you get out of that groove I was talking about. How do we all take a step from where we're stuck, as Cubans? I don't know the answer. I just know that we have to do it right away, because it's been too long.

EDR: So, then I guess you're opposed to the embargo, and, specifically, the more recent restrictions imposed by the U.S. government on Cuban travel.

EM: I think it's horrible. I think it helps keep Fidel in power. I think it's a lesson on how to keep Fidel Castro in power. It makes people scared. It makes Cuban people fear us even more than they already do. It makes them think they don't have a future. The more people that go to Cuba, the quicker Cuba will change. Everybody in Cuba wants change. They're just afraid of us. And the more of us that they meet, the less afraid of us they'll be. I've never met a Cuban who wants to harm another Cuban. I think it's a big mistake, and I'm sorry they keep making the same mistake. And it makes it unbearable for regular people who live there.

EDR: Another one of your plays, *Once Removed*, was produced in Miami and starred Lucie Arnaz. How did the audience react to that?

EM: It was a very interesting experience. People there were very conflicted because it was hard for them to hate a play that Desi Arnaz's daughter was in. I went closing night and sat by myself. In front of me was a Cuban family. The mother was in her seventies. They were loving the play. The play ends with the failure of the Bay of Pigs. About four minutes after that scene, there's a laugh line, and when that laugh line happened, the mother said, "I can't take this. I have to go." And I thought, "She thinks they're laughing at her." And I thought, "It's so real to them still. It's so sad that they can't look at it from even one little perspective away. It's so immediate to them." And I found that very interesting, because this is my "nice" play about Cuba. I can't imagine producing the *Floating Island* plays there. It's so sad, because then how do you and I go further, who had nothing to do with it?

EDR: Don't you think the next generation has?

EM: To some extent, but not completely.

EDR: What do you want your audiences to get out of your plays?

EM: Everything. I want them to know what Cuba is. I went them to make a decision about it. I want them to be moved. I write completely for the audience. You know, there are writers who don't care. I totally care [about the audience], not as individuals, but as a group.

Dionisio Martínez

∴ ∴ ∴

I spent a day with Dionisio Martínez in Tampa, Florida, where he has lived all of his adult life. One of the things I most remember about that day was the rain. The streets of the city were flooded as a result of one of those rare winter thunderstorms. Despite the sudden, booming thunder, Martínez was laid back and relaxed. This contrast stayed with me, perhaps because his poetry, particularly his latest book, Climbing Back, *seems like an exercise in the confluence of disparate elements. Literature, history, philosophy, and jazz all make an appearance as part of the many voices of Martínez's speakers. Because of the intensity and philosophical nature of his poetry, I was pleasantly surprised to encounter the soothing, almost hushed voice with which Martínez speaks, and which is often accompanied by a wry smile or slight chuckle.*

In Bad Alchemy, *Martínez explores the psychological aspects of exile as it relates to such thematic concerns as the fleetingness of life and the ability of memory to distort the truth. His poetry is like a long line of falling dominoes: one image seems to lead to another, which then leads to another. More than emotions connect these images, however; they are linked by the writer's attempt to make sense of an often chaotic world. Even Martínez himself cannot fully explain the thread that connects the seemingly haphazard images in* Bad Alchemy, *he just knows that his job is to create a mythology that lies between the real world and the imaginative one.*

Born in Havana in 1956, Martínez moved to the United States with his family ten years later, after spending a year in Spain. He has read his work at various universities and book festivals, the Academy of American Poets, and the Library of Congress. He has been the recipient of fellowships from the National Endowment for the Arts, the Guggenheim Foundation, and the Whiting Foundation. He is the author of four book-length collections, and his poems have been published individually in over eighty literary magazines and anthologies in the United States and abroad.

In this conversation, Martínez describes the connection between poetry and music, the exilic nature of his verse, and his childhood. The date is February 3, 2006.

Works

Climbing Back (2001)

Bad Alchemy (1995)

History as a Second Language (1993)

Dancing at the Chelsea (1992)

⁖⸍

EDR: You left Cuba at the age of nine. Are there any particular images of those early years that are significant as they apply to your poetry?

DM: One memory that I have is of La Plaza. It was a market. It had everything from a butcher shop, to a little knick-knack store, to a cafeteria. It was right across the street from my grandfather's store. This plaza was part of my life. During my last year in Cuba, they tore it down and made it a park, and so I have several images. One is this very vibrant place where everybody talked at once, and there was business going on. From that image, it changes to the day when they brought trucks and they tied cables to the columns, and slowly all of it came down. So this place, which was very much a part of who I was, was suddenly gone. I remember the night before we left Cuba hearing frogs outside. The sound was coming from this new park, which had replaced the market. The sound of the frogs is an image that has never left me.

EDR: Can you talk a bit about your early years in the United States? Where did you live? What was it like in this different culture? What was your experience adjusting to a new language?

DM: I moved to Glendale, California, to my uncle's house, after living in Spain for about nine months after leaving Cuba. I went to California by myself, and my parents came about two months later. For those two months, I was in a kind of limbo. I had been grounded in Spain. Now, I was pretty much lost. I had to find someone who spoke Spanish just to give me directions to get home from school. I remember walking up and down the streets of Glendale saying, "Do you speaka Spanish?" No one tried to help me. So much time passed that my uncle had to come looking for me [*he laughs*]. That was my first experience with this new language. Another time I remember, this was later, I parked my bike on the playground. This other kid said, "Hello." And I said, "Hello," and we walked into the school. It wasn't until after this happened that I realized that I had had a conversation, simple as it was. It was an epiphany. I could actually understand this new language!

EDR: I know you were influenced by Heberto Padilla.[1] Can you talk a bit about your first exposure to Padilla's work and how that work is present in your own?

DM: He was one of those people who came into my life at a very important moment. I was in my twenties, and I was at the point where I knew I was taking poetry seriously, but I didn't know *where* I was taking it [*he chuckles*]. There was something in the realism of Padilla's poetry that wasn't straightforward journalism. That's where I learned that you could talk about the world as it is, and by mediating just a bit, that thing that would have become just a straight story becomes the poem. Call it invention, or simply lying. He was one of those poets who taught me that the right mediation, the right adjective, the right verb, could take the story from the pedestrian to something much more profound. To me he was terribly, terribly important.

EDR: Since you talk about truth and lying, much of your work deals with the relationship between history and poetry, as one of your books, *History as a Second Language*, attests. How do you see that relationship?

DM: A poem is full of lies, not only because of what it does and how it works, but also because it is often so far removed in time, geographically, and/or psychologically, from the moment you're writing about. Two things are happening with history and poetry. In some cases, we are restoring that which was lost. An example might be the story of La Plaza I told you earlier. Most people might not remember it was torn down. Maybe my job is to bring back that place that was there. In other cases, I think the job of poetry is to create a history within history. To create its own mythology. You're never going to have all the facts, so if you're trying to write that—an "accurate" representation—it's never going to happen. We're not journalists. The wonderful thing about poetry is that it takes from the world of the imagination and [from] the world that is actually there, and it's between those two worlds that the poet creates his own mythology.

EDR: What about your own personal history, and how that informs your poetry? For example, in *Bad Alchemy*, many of the poems begin with an image, or a memory, which then becomes even more personal. The title poem, for example, begins with the [space] shuttle launch, then moves to the death of your father. Is this how you see poetry, as an image that turns inward?

DM: It's like the domino theory. Once you have that trigger—that launching pad, of one thing that leads to another—something else happens. In truth, I'm not sure *what* happens. All I know is I get going, and nothing can stop me. I wrote a poem recently which is three pages long, and it all began with one single image. What happened to get me from point A to point B, and then C, I can't explain. That is one of the wonderful things about art. If we could explain it all, I think it would cease to be art. I think it becomes art often at the point when something else takes over. The ordinary is often the beginning for what I do, and then it's not hard for me to make certain links. What I don't do is try to figure out why or how I do it.

EDR: Many of the poems in *Bad Alchemy*, such as "Fuego," seem to deal with the fleetingness of life, the temporary aspect of it. How everything is, ultimately, an "incomplete combustion," to quote from one of your other poems. Can you comment on this?

DM: Quite simply, what interests me about this notion is the fact that *it*'s there. That "this" is all we have, and what we have is going to disappear. Things disappear while we're still here, and eventually we die. It is the way things are. I could write about how things last, but I am fascinated by the way we survive just about anything. Maybe that's all we have. The fact that we have the power to survive is what we have. There is continuity in some things, but more often than not, there's none. There's a person you knew when you were in your thirties; there's a place you lived at a certain point. All of those things have probably changed. There isn't much continuity.

EDR: Speaking of survival, *Bad Alchemy* is framed by two poems that center on exile. Is that the "bad alchemy" to which you refer, and is that the thread that runs through the entire book?

DM: It's the thread that runs through my life. It runs through anything that I write. I'm not talking about the political but about the psychological aspects of exile. Exile is the one thing that runs through all my books. It's the thing that I talk about and think about. The idea of leaving. The idea that if there *is* continuity, that continuity is just a memory. You are part of a certain place, and even if that place no longer exists, you are still part of it. You don't necessarily detach yourself from places that don't exist. Again, it's not just exile, but the various aspects of it.

EDR: That poem, and perhaps only one or two more in the collection, mention Cuba specifically, yet it can be considered a book of "Cuban-American poetry." Do you feel that's an accurate assessment?

DM: Yes. I think there will always be that outsider in me. I'm more American than anything else, because I've been here longer than anywhere else, and I feel very comfortable where I am. However, there's a part of me that I can't erase. I can't go back in time and be born here. I can't escape that, and I don't want to escape it. I wasn't here for the first ten years of my life, so it's inevitable that when I write, a part of me is somewhere else and on its way here. Then, of course, there's a part of me that's extremely American, closer to the South than to any other place.

EDR: Let's talk about your latest effort, *Climbing Back*. The poems in the book are essentially prose or prose poems. This is an approach you've used before, and you seem to prefer it. Why?

DM: I never give it any thought. I can tell you how the book came about. Again, I can explain what I do, but not *why* I do it. I hadn't realized how many prose poems I'd written over the years, until a couple of years ago, when I was moving things around in preparation for an approaching storm, and I ran across a couple of old notebooks. These were notebooks full of poems that I'd never published or never read again. They were poems that I was hiding somewhere. I had a full manuscript of prose poems. Thankfully, it was never published. I'm not sure how the poems came about. I know I was reading poetry at the time. I was reading the poetry of Ira Sadoff,[2] for instance. I [had] discovered his work when I was in my twenties. He was a big influence. Again, I don't know how exactly those poems came about, but it was at that point, that

I consciously decided to do three things. One was to keep the "prodigal son" theme going. The other was to continue to have this pattern of prose poetry. The third thing was to write it all in the present tense. It just sounded better that way.

EDR: How did you get this idea to connect the biblical story to a series of poems with various speakers?

DM: You were right in something you said earlier, which many people don't get. My poetry begins with something simple, even pedestrian. Those are usually the triggers, and this book was no exception. I was in Spain, and I heard someone make a comment about something, and that comment reminded me of the parable of the prodigal son. The comment itself is irrelevant. The moment I made that connection, everything seemed so natural and obvious. I thought, "Why not have a group of poems where the prodigal son speaks?" While it may not seem like it, there *is* structure there. There is, at least, one poem that's a sestina.[3] The long poem in four sections, called "Credo," is actually a single poem. It is a pantoum.[4] So, there's a circular poem in the middle of the book. The book is also circular in the sense that the last poem in the book is the first poem written backwards. It's circle, within circle, within circle, within circle. I was creating a mythology inside a mythology, inside a mythology. We have the myth of the prodigal son, so why not create my own myth? I thought of it as several speakers. When Jorie Graham[5] picked the book for the National Book Series, she told me something very interesting over the phone. She said, "not only are the speakers different, they're multi-ethnic, multi-national, multi-everything." She's right.

EDR: In a recent NPR interview,[6] you mention that you went to great effort to leave yourself out of the book. Why did you feel that was necessary? Why did you not want to be identified as the prodigal son?

DM: The more I write, the less I write about myself. I thought it would be more effective to have these poems be about him, or them. Although you can detect autobiography, and I can point out things where something in the poem resulted from something in my own life, it's the prodigal son's book. It's not mine. Even in *Bad Alchemy*, there are autobiographical moments that are disconnected. I try to find something larger than an autobiographical connection. If a poem is simply autobiographical, then it becomes a journal entry. I think what makes it more than that is when it is linked to that larger unknown, to that universal thing.

EDR: Ironically, some critics have seen that as the book's flaw.[7] The fact that it is not personal, and therefore not distinctive, as opposed to *Bad Alchemy*. Do you feel it is necessary for Cuban-American writers to explore the theme of exile and loss in their work?

DM: I don't feel I have any obligation to anyone or any community to write a certain way. I write when I have something to say. I find it somewhat humorous when people talk about "community," about "heritage," or about things "they must say." Who said that somebody *must* say something? I don't quite get it. I write. There are parts of my life that happened in Spain, there are parts that happened in California, and parts that happened in places I've visited. A big part of my life I've lived in Florida. All these things in some way make it into my poems. But if I have an obligation to say something as a Cuban, then I have more of an obligation to say something as a Southerner because I've been here longer. I don't think I have an obligation to say anything. I could have been a carpenter. I think writers, like any other artists, have an obligation to do whatever they feel they can do best. If I can communicate certain emotions, do I have to somehow limit it to the fact that I'm Cuban? No.

EDR: What, then, do you feel are the characteristics of Cuban-American literature, if any?

DM: When I read a Cuban writer, I'm not looking for anything other than the fact that I enjoy the novel, the poem, or the short story. I can only tell you what *my* work has. Mine has my Arabic side, because my grandparents came from Lebanon and Syria. I have my Spanish side. My father came from Spain. So, we're talking about people *leaving* their roots before I left mine. There's a lot of leaving in my family. The sense of exile was always a conversation in my life. The whole idea of uprooting, starting from scratch, my father's stories about how he made his way to Cuba. My personal poetry contains all of those fragmented lives before mine. To me, that's part of what my writing does. The one thing that defines it [is] the many ways to look at exile. Geographical distance, emotional distance, and psychological distance. For Cuban-American poetry, or literature in general, I think there are many threads. I don't think there's any *one* picture or theme. Each writer has to find his or her way into the page, and a way into the reader with that unique voice. Ultimately, that's all we have. The moment you consider yourself a Cuban writer, or a Southern writer, or a woman writer, that uniqueness is gone. That doesn't mean you're not a Cuban, or a Southerner, or a woman.

You are one, or three, or ten of those things, by default. The moment you *try* to become one of those things, then there is less and less of you. The one thing above all that each writer has is his voice.

EDR: Currently, you've been integrating your poetry with music. What is the connection you see between the two?

DM: Poetry *is* music. Along with not just telling a straight story with poetry, a poet can't be afraid of getting lost. Cubans are always looking for a sense of place, but an artist, almost by definition, is incomplete and lost. If an artist were complete and perfect, and knew where he was headed, he would be an accountant. Poetry is a journey of discovery.

Pablo Medina

⁘ ⁘ ⁘

Pablo Medina is one of the most versatile writers included in this collection. He is a novelist, short-story writer, poet, and essayist. Among his longer works are Exiled Memories: A Cuban Childhood, The Marks of Birth, The Floating Island, *and* The Cigar Roller. *Dozens of his shorter works have been published in academic journals and popular magazines throughout the United States. He has lived most of his life in the Northeast since he emigrated from Cuba with his family at the age of twelve.*

Pablo Medina's poetry is much like his fiction: unassuming yet powerful. Pork Rind and Cuban Love Songs *(1975) was the first book of poetry written in English by a Cuban-born writer. In it, Medina presents the reader with poems, like "The Exile," that depict the speaker's connection to the past, a staple of Cuban-American literature. What is not typical, however, is Medina's powerful use of imagery: visual, auditory, and tactile.*

Two of his novels, The Return of Felix Nogara *and* The Marks of Birth, *center around characters who long to return to Cuba. Nogara's return is marked by political upheaval, but ultimately, he finds contentment in the land he left behind many years ago. For Antón, the main character in* The Marks of Birth, *his birthmark has never let him forget his ancestral home. He returns to Cuba with his grandmother's ashes, and like Nogara, he seems to find a fulfillment he had never achieved in his adopted country. Like these two fictional characters, in* Exiled Memories, *Medina recounts his own journey back to Cuba after a long absence. Unlike his characters, however, in this autobiographical work, Medina reveals a persona whose self can never be reconciled. It is a persona that does not correspond to the composed and self-assured writer with whom I am conversing.*

As we sit in his office at The New School in Manhattan, however, it strikes me that the tone of Medina's work reflects the man himself. Although not a large man in stature, Medina's engaging and easygoing manner immediately commands attention. In addition to talking about his work, Medina addresses such issues as bilingualism, labeling, and exile. He also describes his experience when he returned to Cuba after a thirty-eight-year absence. The date is July 20, 2004.[1]

Works

The Cigar Roller (2005)

Points of Balance/Puntos de apoyo (2005)

Puntos de apoyo (2002)

The Return of Felix Nogara (2000)

The Floating Island (1999)

The Marks of Birth (1994)

Arching into the Afterlife (1991)

Exiled Memories: A Cuban Childhood (1990/2005)

Everyone Will Have to Listen: The Poetry of Tania Díaz (translator, with Carolina Hospital, 1990)

Pork Rind and Cuban Songs (1975)

·:·

EDR: I'd like to start with your first book of poems, *Pork Rind and Cuban Songs.* That book is touted as the first collection of verse written in English by a Cuban-American. Why did you decide to write exclusively in English?

PM: Well, I do also write in Spanish, but you're right, most of it is in English. Right now, I'm making notes in Spanish for the novel I plan to work on after the one I'm working on now. I would like to write that book in Spanish.

EDR: Why?

PM: Because my sensibility in Spanish is very different from my sensibility in English. I am generally pleased with the novels that I've written in English. Not 100 percent, because no one is ever 100 percent pleased with anything one writes, but I'm fairly satisfied. But I do have this other language inside of me, which compels me. I am driven to find it inside my literature. After all, it's the language that I use on a daily basis, and it's the language that I read constantly. So, why should it be closeted away, and why shouldn't I use it as a medium for my writing?

EDR: So, then, why did you write exclusively in English when you first started writing?

PM: When I first started writing, I started writing in Spanish. Then, I switched to English. Then, for a while, I was writing in both languages. Nicanor Parra[2] had a workshop at Columbia University, and he invited me there. I came and I read some Spanish poems and some English poems. And afterward, we were gathered somewhere having a cup of coffee, and he said, "You're going to have to choose a language." I said, "I don't know, I might keep writing in both." But I chose English for reasons that have to do with the fact that again, English was the language that surrounded me on a daily basis. I was studying English literature, so I felt immersed in English literature. I felt immersed in the language of English literature. I put Spanish aside and didn't come back to it in my writing until the mid-'90s in a serious way.

EDR: So, what you said earlier about choosing a language, you did back then, but is it still true?

PM: Well, I think that, at some point, there comes a choice, and that choice is dictated by a number of factors. If a piece of writing comes out, say, in Spanish, well, the fact that you thought it in Spanish, that you wrote it in Spanish, whether a page or two or twenty, is telling you something about where it came from inside you. If it comes [out] in English, then it's the same. This last novel, *The Cigar Roller*, whole chunks of it were written in Spanish.

EDR: And parts of it are appearing in Spanish?

PM: No, because then you have to make a conscious decision as to who is going to read a novel, parts of which are in Spanish, and parts in English.

EDR: This novel deals with the Cuban cigar rollers of Tampa and Ybor City. How did you become interested in this topic?

PM: On visiting relatives who had moved to Tampa, I was taken on a drive through Ybor City. Though I knew about the *tampeños* from my readings, being in the place where they lived and thrived for a time was the spark that led to my researching the Cuban experience in Tampa, which predated and anticipated the present exile.

EDR: What kind of research did you do to feel you could write about this period in the Cuban-American experience?

PM: Not a lot has been written about the Cubans in Tampa, but there are some interesting texts, notably Gary Mormino and George Pozzetta's *The Immigrant World of Ybor City*, as well as books by José Yglesias and Ferdie Pacheco, both of whom grew up in Tampa.[3] There are a number of scholarly articles on the subject—I recall those by Gerald Pozo and Louis Pérez—as well as unpublished dissertations. The University of South Florida has a collection of unpublished materials dealing with Ybor City. It is a treasure trove of letters, menus dating from the early twentieth century, even grocery lists, that I found truly fascinating. Also in that collection are a number of interviews of cigar workers done by WPA writers during the Depression. I personally interviewed a number of old-timers, many of whom gathered at La Tropicana cafeteria every morning for *café con leche*. The late Tony Piso, the official historian of Tampa, and Adela Gonzmart, late owner of the Columbia Restaurant, provided a great deal of information. Between the whistle and the flute, the research took about fifteen years, but during much of that time, I was working on other books.

EDR: Is Amadeo's fate some type of punishment for his pursuit of earthly pleasures?

PM: Absolutely not. There are many good saintly people who suffer similar fates at the end of their lives. Amadeo Terra's fate is that of all human beings: we get sick and we die, sometimes miserably, no matter how virtuous we may have been.

EDR: Are you pleased with the Spanish translation of the novel? Did you work with the translator? Is anything lost in translation?

PM: It is okay, though the novel has acquired a Mexican tinge to it, as it was translated and published in Mexico. I had an opportunity to edit the translation. Much is lost in translation and much is gained.

EDR: You said earlier that a writer must make a choice to write either in Spanish or English. Some Latino authors though, most notably Chicano poets, do publish works in both languages.

PM: Yes, but I've never done anything like that. The poems that are going to appear in Spanish next year are not translations. They're appearing one in English, followed by one in Spanish.[4]

EDR: Let's switch from the language within the work to the language that is used to identify people, especially Latino authors. How do you feel about labels? About being labeled a Cuban-American poet, for instance?

PM: About labels, in general, I don't like them. I am very uncomfortable with them because they're labels that come not as a way of clarifying literature, but as a way of putting literature into a neat category. They're extra-literary. And I wonder to what degree they're created by literary critics, or sociologists, or whomever.

EDR: How about yourself personally? How do you identify yourself to others?

PM: I call myself a Cuban-born writer.

EDR: Why do you hyphenate that? Why not just Cuban?

PM: Well, because I write in English, and if I don't say Cuban-born . . . I don't want to leave that part of me behind.

EDR: Do you see yourself that way?

PM: When it comes down to saying it, I'm Cuban. And the term Cuban-American, I don't know who thought that up. The term Cuban-American for me is redundant for two reasons. One, it's redundant in a hemispheric sense, because all Cubans are Americans. And secondly, to be Cuban culturally is, I think, to embrace whatever historic connections there have been between the United States and Cuba. They're impossible to ignore. They're impossible to push aside, and I think they're very deeply ingrained in the Cuban psyche.

EDR: But it's not redundant in the way Puerto Rican American is redundant, in that there, by definition, you're an American.

PM: Yes, I can see a term like Nuyorican[5] being much more accurate than Puerto Rican American.

EDR: In the new edition of *Exiled Memories*, you discuss this issue of labeling and identity with your son. Specifically, you ask him where home is, and he says, "New York." You then write that you're not sure what the answer to that question is for yourself. Has that changed since then?

PM: No. I don't feel at home anywhere. I mean by home some place that nurtured you in your growing years. I don't feel nurtured by any place where I have been outside of Cuba. But the paradox comes when you go back to Cuba, and you realize that Cuba is no longer the Cuba of your nurturing. It's some place totally different. So, even that place of nurturing does not exist.

EDR: Is that why your characters, Antón, Felix Nogara, even your own persona, long to return to Cuba, but when they do, their lives are not fulfilled?

PM: In a sense, Felix Nogara was fulfilled. He became a taxi driver, he married this girl, and he grew old and died. How much more fulfillment can there be? He went back to where he wanted to be. Despite politics, despite everything else, that's where he wanted to go. And that's where he lives the rest of his life. That's fulfillment. His disappointments are part of life, and he keeps living.

EDR: How much of you is in Felix Nogara, especially after your own return to Cuba?

PM: Let me answer that by not answering it. As I've developed as a novelist, my characters become less and less outwardly like myself but driven by the same things that drive me.

EDR: In *Exiled Memories*, you also write that if you didn't return to Cuba, then you might never return. Can you explain that?

PM: Well, the age of fifty is crucial because you're no longer a young man, you're about to enter maturity. The things that you've wanted to do that you haven't done begin to weigh very heavily on you. For me, the primary thing that I hadn't done that I wanted to do was go back. Not in any political sense, not in any sense of wanting to see the wreckage of the revolution or even the triumph of the revolution, if I wanted to think that way. But simply to go back. Not to see family, because most of my family there had died or had left the island, and not to see friends. Because of how symbolic fifty is, it was imperative to do so, and if I hadn't followed that imperative, I would've felt defeated and probably would not have gone back.

EDR: You write about this trip in *Exiled Memories*, particularly about not finding the things you remembered from your childhood, or finding things changed dramatically, like your house.

PM: It was a very difficult, complicated, anxiety-laden trip. Even though you expect something like that to happen, when you're actually there and noticing the particulars and the details of how it looks, it's very different than anticipating it. You realize how much of that life has been walled off that you can't reenter. The irony; the dark irony. A beautiful, airy home. A relatively large, relatively new home that had been turned into a moldy wreckage of those aspirations that led to the building of it.

EDR: You also write about being questioned at the airport in Havana, much like Felix Nogara was.

PM: When you enter a situation like that, of course, it's the stuff of nightmares. I thought that it might happen, but when it actually does, you don't know what the outcome might be. My concern was trying to soften and ease the situation as much as possible, because I didn't want to harm my son in any way. I didn't want him to be affected by this. I didn't want to get into any kind of conflict or argument that appeared to me to be with relatively minor officials in this room. I had nothing to gain. I surprised myself at how cool I was. It was only later, as we were driving into the city, that my leg started shaking. But in the process, I was extremely cool. I even offered the guy a piece of candy. And he took it. So, I may not have been aware of it then, but at some level, his taking the candy meant that we were going to be allowed out of there.

EDR: Since you mention that this candy seemed somehow symbolic, let me ask you about your first novel, *The Marks of Birth*. This idea, that the mark on Antón's body seems symbolic, was it influenced by Hawthorne, since your degree is in American literature?

PM: It actually came from a mark that my grandmother had on her back and my son inherited. But it was a little heavy-handed in that book. If I were to write it now, I would diminish it. But you know, it was my first novel, and it was a learning experience as much as anything else.

EDR: Another symbol that appears in that book and that seems to recur in your novels is the blond, blue-eyed woman. What can you tell me about that?

PM: It's a figure of longing, and it's a figure of desire for *The Other*, *The Different One*. I played with that throughout.

EDR: Why does Antón come to the fate that he does?

PM: Well, he disappears, and he re-appears in *The Return of Felix Nogara* as a minor character. So his life doesn't end.

EDR: Did you have that in mind when you ended the novel? That he would return?

PM: No. What I had in mind was, I have to end this book, and how I am going to end it? [*He chuckles.*] There are certain demands that are placed upon a novelist, and you have to meet those demands. I imagine I could have ended it any other way. The fact that he takes his grandmother's ashes back, at that point, is the best he could do in terms of return. I imagine a critic might say that somehow reflects personally on the author, that, at that time, that was the best he could do. By the way, that theme of flying under the radar, I wrote that theme before the incident involving the Cuban pilot who returned to Cuba to pick up his wife and daughters and landed on a highway outside Havana.[6]

EDR: Let's switch to poetry once again. *Arching into the Afterlife* is a departure from your previous works. It's been described as "angry" and been compared to Eliot's *The Wasteland*. Why the shift from Cuban "songs" to this darker series of poems?

PM: A lot of those poems were written in places where I lived or knew very well that could be labeled a sort of industrial wasteland. Newark, New Jersey, Trenton. . . . To some degree those poems represent and reflect the idea of the wasteland. Although Eliot was there in bits and pieces, I wasn't consciously alluding to him.

EDR: What other writers do you think inspired you?

PM: You're always inspired and molded by the writers you're reading at the time. I'm a very eclectic reader. I don't set a reading list for myself, or a studied pattern of reading. But there are some writers. There's Alejo Carpentier,[7] whose work I've been close to. There's García Marquez,[8] whose work I've been close to, but who isn't close to García Marquez? But I feel closer, in terms of sensibility, to Carpentier. I'm talking fiction as opposed to poetry. Another writer I've been reading is José Saramago.[9] He's an extraordinary writer. I just finished reading *A History of the Siege of Lisbon*, which is an incredible book. And I feel somehow engaged with those writers as I was with Faulkner, as I was with Hemingway and Fitzgerald, and Mark Twain. Especially Mark Twain. Mark Twain is as good a novelist as the United States has produced. Hemingway said there's nobody better.

EDR: Back to *Arching*. There's very little about Cuba in it.

PM: Yes, it's not that I wasn't thinking about it. Poetry, for me, is a spontaneous reaction.

EDR: Sounds like Wordsworth.

PM: Yes, recollected in tranquility. Part of being a poet is allowing yourself to be exposed to the environment, and then responding. At the time, I was responding as an individual living in places that were not very satisfying for me. Living in circumstances that were not very positive for me, and much of that is reflected in the vibration of the poems in the book.

EDR: What about the lilacs in bloom at the book's conclusion?

PM: That was my attempt to write some sort of Whitmanesque liberation of the industrial landscape. I don't know if it worked or not. It was my feeble attempt to do that.

EDR: In your next book of poetry, *The Floating Island*, you return to Cuba. You also write extensively about Miami, but as a place where the speaker doesn't feel quite comfortable.

PM: You're right. Again, the environment provided the initial impetus to write the poems, but it was my own discomfort with that environment that completed them.

EDR: I think many people would find that ironic. A Cuban who doesn't feel comfortable in Miami.

PM: It is ironic. Miami is a very closed city. It's a very polarized city. There are very well-defined groups, and those groups tend not to interact. Or if they interact, they do so for political gain or in conflict. There's the African-American group, there's what they call the Anglo group, there's the Haitian group, and then there's the Cuban group. Of course there are other groups, and I'm oversimplifying the situation. But they all seem to be in conflict; they don't seem to meld or join together. When you come in from the outside and you try to become comfortable, or try to connect with at least one of those groups, it is impossible. And I was used to connecting with a number of different groups, because I came from New York, where you necessarily connect with any number of groups that are around you. The groups in Miami protect themselves by becoming very enclosed. They say, "Well, you're Cuban, you go to the Cuban group," or "Well, you're from New York, you're a liberal New Yorker." So, you never quite can get in because of that polarization, and I found that was very difficult to crack. I felt more of a foreigner in Miami than I felt anywhere else.

EDR: You obviously feel comfortable in this city now, but what was it like when you first arrived here at the age of twelve?

PM: New York is a unique place. It's a place that struggles with your imagination. Anything you can try to imagine is less than the reality that surrounds you here. That was my experience when I arrived in New York. I've also written elsewhere that it helped me that I grew up in Havana the first twelve years. I think there are a lot of parallels between a city like Havana and a city like New York. So, I didn't feel that uncomfortable. Besides, there was a precedent, and there was a history of Cubans being in New York from the eighteenth century on, [people] who lived here for many years, including writers like Cirilo Villaverde, who lived here close to forty years. There was José Marti. Also, Félix Varela, who ministered to the Irish in Lower Manhattan. So, there is a sense in which this is not unknown territory for Cubans.[10]

EDR: I'd like to switch for a minute to discuss the broader issue of Cuban-American literature. One of the things I hope to accomplish is to define this field. What would you say are its characteristics?

PM: I think that bad Cuban-American literature becomes mired in nostalgia. I think it was Cabrera Infante[11] who called nostalgia the bastard child of memory. I think bad Cuban-American literature falls into that category. The best Cuban-American literature forces a confrontation with the whole concept of displacement, as a condition and as a point in which you function. I guess you could call that the exilic condition; that you learn to live in a space which lies between two cultures. Pérez Firmat calls it "life on the hyphen."[12] I like to think of it more as a parenthesis.

EDR: Can you explain that?

PM: The hyphen is divisive. The parenthesis implies a space between.

EDR: But a hyphen also joins.

PM: But I'm talking about a space. It's not divided. It's not joined. It's just a space.

EDR: And that space in which the individual lives embodies a conflict which is never resolved?

PM: It probably isn't ever resolved. But you can learn, I hope, to live in that space, in a fruitful way. I'm thinking of Nabokov as a paradigm for that kind of situation.[13] He not only lived in it, he flourished in it as a writer. Heberto Padilla used to tell me "I'm not interested in what happens to you at four in the morning. I'm interested in how it functions in your literature."[14]

EDR: Is that what happened to Felix Nogara? He never learned to live in that space?

PM: Exactly. If he had, he would have never needed to return. But for those of us who remain here and will probably remain here for the rest of our lives, learning to live in that space is very important.

EDR: But you write in *Exiled Memories* that you might someday return to Cuba and perhaps stay there.

PM: Well, you write what you long for at one moment, but in more measured moments, you realize that may not happen. What's really interesting to think about is what's going to happen to those of us who identify ourselves as exiles in this country, when exile is no longer an issue.

Achy Obejas

photograph by Ovie Carter

∴ ∴ ∴

Of all the conversations in this book, this was perhaps the most difficult to edit. Achy Obejas's passion for her work is confirmed when she speaks of it. Her enthusiasm often results in discourse that leads in many different directions. Her novels reflect this variety. They are rich in characters with diverse sexual orientations, multi-ethnic backgrounds, and wide-ranging socioeconomic levels. Her ability to create this multiplicity may be a result of her journalistic training, as well as many years of residency in Chicago, one of the country's most diverse cities.

Obejas was born in Havana in 1956, and she came to the United States with her family when she was six years old. She grew up in Michigan City, Indiana, and in 1979, she moved to Chicago, where she has lived ever since. She has written for several newspapers, including the Chicago Sun-Times, The Advocate, *and* The Village Voice. *Currently, she writes for the* Chicago Tribune, *and she teaches creative writing at DePaul University in Chicago.*

Her collection of short stories We Came All the Way from Cuba So You Could Dress Like This? *contains many aspects of Obejas's own experiences, including a fictionalized account of her family's journey to America. Her creative interest in the way memory distorts history continues in her much acclaimed first novel,* Memory Mambo. *Juani, the central figure, is both attracted to and repulsed by one of the book's male characters. In this fashion, Obejas employs a lesbian Cuban-American to both confront and reject her own identity. This precarious balancing act of conflicting identity continues in her next work,* Days of Awe. *Again drawing from her own background, Obejas adds a religious dimension to the stigma of being a marginalized and conflicted gay Cuban exile. As occurs in all her works, the central character, a young woman named Alejandra, attempts and eventually achieves inner cohesion. The healing power of forgiveness that the novel espouses is what Obejas desires for all Cubans, regardless of political persuasion.*

Her individual stories have appeared in numerous literary journals and anthologies. An accomplished poet, she received an NEA poetry fellowship in 1986. Additionally, Days of Awe *received the Lambda Award for Lesbian Fiction in 2002.*

This conversation took place in New York City on June 6, 2005, during the Cuban Congress Conference on Literature.

Works

This Is What Happened in Our Other Life (2007)

Havana Noir (2007)

Days of Awe (2001)

Memory Mambo (1996)

We Came All the Way from Cuba So You Could Dress Like This? (1994)

∴

EDR: Let's start with your collection of short stories, *We Came All the Way from Cuba So You Could Dress Like This?* What prompted you to put together a collection?

AO: I had the feeling that I wanted to finish stories that I ran into during my daily life as a journalist. As a journalist, you usually meet someone during a crisis, and you want to find an ending that has some sort of resolution. As a journalist, you don't always get to do that. So I started all these stories, but I wasn't finishing them. I was going from headline to headline. Then, I decided I would go back to school. One of the things I did there was polish a lot of these stories. When I went to the *Chicago Sun Times* in 1980, precisely what they were interested in were some of the things that I was interested in, which was the Latino community. The Latino community at that time was going through a period of tremendous flux. The city government was a long-time corrupt machine. The *Sun Times*, which was then a progressive blue-collar paper, was putting together a section in Spanish, and I was hired as one of the writers there. It was a terrific experience. From there, I went back to the alternative press, where I had done some work before, which at that point was perfect for me because I got to write in English for a wider audience. There was a lot of activity and a lot of madness in the gay community in Chicago. The AIDS crisis was going on. It seemed like my life was surrounded by urgency. I was writing a lot. I had a lot to say. So, making the jump to fiction was not difficult at all. I was also very lucky in that my editors were interested in my literary voice.

EDR: Only one of those stories, the title one, deals explicitly with Cuban exile. How do you see the collection as a whole as a work of Cuban-American literature?

AO: Well, the book is not about Cuban-Americans. It's about Chicago. What ties the stories together are adventures in Chicago. Chicago is a city unlike any other city in the United States, in terms of the Latino population. It's not overwhelmed by any one group. You know how New York is pretty much overwhelmed by Puerto Ricans, Miami by Cubans, and Los Angeles by Mexicans? Chicago just doesn't work that way, especially in the 1980s. In the '80s Chicago had about three or four hundred thousand Mexicans, and about a quarter of a million Puerto Ricans, and a very strong representation from a variety of other groups. The Cubans had a real presence, which they don't have now. The Guatemalans had a real presence, which they increased. There's a theater group, for example, who are all Latinas. They sold tee-shirts after their first show with names on them that sort of really captured this whole spirit of bizarre integration we have in Chicago in the Latino community. It said things like Chicano-Riqueño, Guaterican, Mexiyorian, etc. It hyphenated, and merged, and fused all these different Latino identities. I know the book sells as a Cuban-American thing, and I'm glad it did. I mean, I *am* Cuban-American. But my intent was to write a book whose scenes were connected by the city. It's a city that I really love, and it's a city that I'm still fascinated by.

EDR: An integral part of your work, which first surfaces in these stories, is homosexuality. One of those stories, "Above All, a Family Man," not only deals with the issue of homophobia but also with the devastating effect of AIDS on our humanity, our humanness. Why was that such an important subject for you?

AO: Well, in the '80s, most of my friends were dying. There was a tremendous focus in my life on the gay community because I was very involved with the AIDS crisis. I was working for an activist newspaper as a freelancer. I was surrounded by a lot of gay men, and I was very close to a lot of gay men. It was also a time when AIDS was very new, and people didn't understand much about it. The very beginning of AIDS education really drew some lines about how culturally different Latinos are from Whites. I mean different in terns of how sexual identity is perceived and identified. I mean, if a White guy does it with another gay, top or bottom, it doesn't really matter, he's queer. That doesn't necessarily play in the Latino community. Whether you're top or bottom defines your identity. It's much more fluid, and it's much more elastic. I was kind of engaged in all this stuff, and thinking about this stuff all the time. That story was meant to be an outreach story or an education story. Of course it was also meant to be literature, but it came from that experience.

EDR: How does that facet of your work play in Cuba? What is the situation there for the gay community?

AO: Cuban society functions on three different levels. One is the personal level, which has nothing to do with what the revolutionary attitude might be. If you're liked, they put up with you. My Cuban girlfriend, Tania, and I break a lot of rules. The general attitude is [that] you can be as queer as you want, as long as you don't talk about it. You can function queerly. In Cuba, people don't marry to have beards, or cover up, or whatever. People function queerly, and everybody understands who's queer and who's not. You just don't acknowledge it, which is, of course, a completely unnatural state of being. Imagine going through your life never once acknowledging your wife is your wife. As I said, Tania and I do acknowledge it. We do things like hold hands in public. We're allowed that for a number of reasons. One, because we're girls. If we were boys, we'd never get away with it. Secondly, because we have male friends who, I think, feel that it speaks well of them, that two attractive lesbians like them. Three, because we're light skinned, and we each independently have a certain status. I'm not sure it would be allowed if we worked at the corner *bodega*.

EDR: The title story in that collection recounts the character's escape from Cuba, which is very similar to your own. Can you talk about that experience, and what part of it, like in *Memory Mambo*, is your own or a borrowed memory?

AO: I don't know what I own and what's a borrowed memory on that one. That's a real complicated one. There was a time when I told the story, and I didn't know what I was going to say. And then, after a certain period of time, you know, you polish the public version of the story, and that sort of becomes your statement on it. You add and subtract for different reasons. It's not an invention. It's emphasis. I've tried to reconstruct and deconstruct that story a number of times. And there've been times when I've stopped and reconsidered what it is that really happened. What I know—what doesn't change ever—is that it was my parents' decision. I was six and a half. We left Cuba on a twenty-eight-foot boat. There were forty-four of us. We were picked up by an oil tanker midway thru the journey, and we were taken to Miami. We left Cuba [on] February 10, 1963. We arrived in American waters a minute after midnight, February 12, which is Lincoln's birthday, which my father found symbolically important [*she laughs*]. Of the forty-four, seventeen were kids. It was total darkness at night time. There was sea sickness. There was a tremendous amount of numbing fear. There was a lot of praying. I remember when we drew up against the oil tanker. I remember the rope ladder. I remember my dad pushing me up on the rope ladder, and we were sort of scooped up and dropped on the deck by American sailors. They were red skinned. They had tattoos. We had never seen anything like it in our lives. I don't think we had seen Americans before.

EDR: When you arrived in the U.S., you lived briefly in Miami, but then moved to Indiana. What was it like growing up a Latina in a Midwest setting?

AO: We were part of a huge group of re-settled Cubans. It was a program under what was then the Housing Education and Welfare Department resettlement program designed to keep Cubans from concentrating in Miami. That was brilliant! [*She laughs heartily.*] They were sending Cubans out to places like Iowa, Indiana, Nevada, Wyoming. We all lived together in the same dormitory. There was a teaching shortage, so they were retraining all these Cuban professionals to become Spanish teachers. So, my mom and dad got into the program. That whole time there was kind of surreal. There were one hundred and fifty families all living in a dorm. Nobody really spoke English. Everybody was on some sort of public assistance. There were maybe four cars for the entire tribal unit there. So, every time you did something, you had to do it en masse. Everything was very collectively oriented. It was a year of tremendous learning.

EDR: Since you bring up the issue of English, let's talk about language. While many of your characters often use Spanish words, they speak and think mostly in English. How difficult was it for you growing up to acquire this new language?

AO: My mom got a job in Michigan City, which is a terrific little town right on the lake. That's when we first started encountering English and really having to contend with it. My dad was very much a purist. He really believed we would go back to Cuba, and he was adamant that we should be able to function in Cuba, so we had to function in Spanish. And we couldn't just know rudimentary Spanish. And we couldn't mix it up. We would hear other Latinos in the United States speaking in Spanish after they'd been here a while, and my dad was absolutely horrified. He was one of those Cuban guys who had a much stronger identification with Spain than he ever did with the African diasporic aspect of the island. He idealized and romanticized Spain a great deal. It was really important for him that we speak good Spanish. In fact, he sent me to Mexico to school two summers in a row so that I would practice my Spanish. I didn't really use Spanglish in any day-to-day way until I got to Chicago. I didn't grow up code-switching. I grew up speaking in English or in Spanish.

EDR: Do you think that English is one of the requirements of Cuban-American literature?

AO: They ask the reverse of that in Cuba all the time. They don't know what to do with writers like me, or Cristina [García][1] because we write in English. But they want to claim us in some way. And they've got all these arbitrary rules about language. My sense is that language is not static, and your use of language is not static. You use what you need at the time. It makes sense to me that most Cuban-American writing would be in English, because the writers who are creating that literature are people who, for the most part, have been educated in the United States. And I think that's the key. It's not that people are bilingual, or culture dominant, or whatever, but, more specifically, that they're educated in the United States, so this becomes the language that we're comfortable with. There's also a vocabulary of identity crisis in English that doesn't exist in the same developed state in Spanish. Not to suggest that we don't have the identity crisis in Latin America, but when you're in Latin America, you don't spend a whole lot of time defining yourself as Latin American. Countries that feel their national identity somewhat threatened is where you have these gigantic discourses about nationality. The whole language of the hyphenated identity happens when you get to the United States and you end up existing among so many different worlds. So, this is the language in which you are having formal intellectual conversations. This is the language of school, of business, of trade. So it becomes the language in which you function.

EDR: In addition to sexuality, a focus on distorted memory is also an integral part of your work. Would you say that this is another component of Cuban-American literature?

AO: It is in my own work. The things that make my own work really different are at least two. One is the sexuality. I certainly do create gay characters and examine those kinds of relationships, but the sexuality is integrated into the story. My stories are not gay stories. They're not Latino stories. They're both. The other thing that I do, that I haven't seen anyone else do, is talk about Latinos, but not as a particular group. I read Cristina [García], and she's talking about Cubans. I read Sandra [Cisneros],[2] and she's talking about Mexicans. I read Tato Laviera,[3] and he's talking about Puerto Ricans. You read my books, and all of those people are in my life. I think it's much more realistic. Most of us do not function in a Cuban-only world, or Puerto Rican–only world, or a gay-only world. That's ridiculous. One of the things that I despise about a lot of gay literature is that the stories create universes where everybody is gay, except of course the bad guy, the straight white guy [she laughs]. I just don't know where that world is, because even in the deepest, ugliest ghetto, at some point, you must interact with the rest of the world, especially if you're living in the city. You have to know other people, unless you never leave your block. I'm not saying it's impossible, but for most of us, it's not true. When I read people like Sandra or Cristina, I think, "This is not my life; my life is much more diverse than this." I don't know if these are choices they make for spiritual reasons, or commercial reasons, or whatever. I have no clue, but I think the world is much more complicated than that.

EDR: Let's talk about the use of memory in your own work, then, specifically [about] Memory Mambo. Juani remembers her father's stories, such as the one where he invented duct tape, for instance, and feels a need to dispel them. Why is that so important for her?

AO: A lot of that comes from a personal experience I had. My dad was always telling us these fantastic stories, where he was always the hero. Yet, when you saw him function in the world, it didn't make sense, because he was certainly not a leader of men, even among his domino-playing

Cuban buddies. He was more a follower of men. He was very principled, and he didn't budge or let himself be swayed, but he was not really a man of action. But in these stories, he was always the leader in terms of action, and I always had doubts about them growing up. The mild-mannered guy that I knew as my dad didn't match this heroic figure. The stories were usually about him and the counterrevolution: he was hiding weapons, or getting people out of the country. Nothing suggested that he was that wily. Then things would happen that would make me question my doubts. For example, once I was in a dentist's office in Miami, and the receptionist called my name, and then she said, "Are you Pepe Obejas's daughter?" Then she said, "Your dad saved my life." And I thought "What? My mild-mannered father saved your life?" It turns out my father planned the trip that got her out of Cuba. For Juani, then, it's an identity issue. Am I the daughter of a hero, or the daughter of a great storyteller? It makes a difference, I think, in how you view yourself.

EDR: Can you explain the relationship that Juani has with Jimmy. How is their relationship related to the concept of fragmented memory?

AO: Often we're attracted to things that we're afraid of. She's attracted to Jimmy's power. I think she's attracted to his possibilities, and what's not available to her. He's a man, and he's straight; she's a girl, and she's not straight. Everything about him is on the table; very little about her is on the table. I think that one of the things that happens, in terms of their relationship and memory, is that sometimes really big events are blinding. They're so traumatizing that you really don't know what happened. People often see what they want. She has a tremendous affinity with Jimmy. He resonates with her. When he commits this terrible, terrible act, it asks questions about her. Therefore, it's much better not to have seen it that well. It's much better not to remember it correctly. To ponder it means to consider what the possibilities are in you, where the evil is in you.

EDR: Juani seems obsessed with her lover, Gina. Why does Juani react violently to her the way she does?

AO: I think she's angry with a lot of people she's not going to confront. Gina is kind of a blank slate. She's considering who she is. Who she might be. Who she could be. This blindness, or selective memory, is related to the Cuban-American condition. One of the things that's really interesting about Cuban-Americans is that there is not a lot of freedom to explore the Cuban part of that dynamic, outside specific cultural situations.

There isn't a whole lot of room, for example, to explore and question the most important influence in all of our lives: the revolution. There is not a whole lot of room within the whole Cuban-American mentality, although it's changing, to question a whole lot of things about the revolution. I'm not talking about good or bad. I'm talking about how it works, how it functions, in terms of how it affects people. It's interesting to me, because I'm involved with someone who lives in Cuba, who's also learning how to deal with that issue outside of the revolutionary process. For example, you never really question why we came to the United States: "We all came to get away from a terrible tyrannical society." Really? Is that why we *all* came? Nobody ever came because it was a good excuse, because they always wanted to come to the United States? Nobody ever came because Cuba was *not* a pre-socialist paradise? Nobody ever came because they wanted greater freedom than what was offered in pre-revolutionary Cuba? Nobody ever came because they were sick of the Third World? Nobody ever came because of economic opportunity? Nobody ever came for any other reason? Everybody came for political and philosophical reasons? We were all that pure? Give me a break! I'm not questioning that politics was part of the package. That was certainly the impetus, but I don't believe we were all that pure. To question that, though, is to question our parents' reality. That's the foundation of their life here. Without the revolution, some of us would have come anyway, and some of us would have stayed in Cuba wishing we were here. Therefore, there's a myth in the Cuban-American community about who we are. We're the "golden exiles." We work harder than everyone else, and we should be privileged in some way. Why do we deserve the Cuban Readjustment Act?[4] What makes our situation different than the Haitian one, for example? Why can't we question that?

EDR: In addition to sexuality and memory, a third component of your work is exile. Many Cuban-American writers point to the issue of exile as this literature's defining characteristic. Do you agree?

AO: I don't think that's necessary. I think it's a defining aspect of Cuban-American literature in *this* generation. I'm not so sure that's going to be true the next time out. This is where Gustavo [Pérez Firmat][5] is correct. This is a unique moment in terms of Cuban-American history. There is a bridging generation. A generation that functions in English and Spanish that may have some memories of its own—or may have some borrowed memories of a very immediate nature about the home country—and yet functions in this country pretty effortlessly. I wonder, twenty years from now, who the Cuban-American writers will be. Most of them will be born in the United States, will barely know Spanish, and will have no sense of themselves as exiles at all. I think there are even people in *my* generation who are already moving very much away from that, and see Cuba more and more as an idea. And soon it will be Cuba as an echo. An echo in the same way that Irish-American literature, or Jewish-American literature is. It will have more affinity to something like that, than it will to Puerto Rican or Mexican-American literature.

EDR: For now, though, your own work incorporates many elements from the Puerto Rican community. In *Memory Mambo*, for instance, there are several Puerto Rican characters. Clearly, there are similarities between Cuban and Puerto Rican culture, but how do you think their literature differs?

AO: Puerto Rican literature has two constants that we do not have, and we *will* not have. One is the going back and forth between the island and the United States. Puerto Ricans come and go. There is a divorce for us from our island. As we stay in this country longer, that divorce will become more distant. You can only be traumatized for so long. The other thing is that I think Puerto Ricans, because of their colonial status (I know it's a Commonwealth, but as far as I'm concerned, it's a colonial status) are politically and psychologically in a place that we're not, and that good or bad, the revolution has erased. Cubans are very nationalistic, whether they're here or on the island, or in Paris, or wherever. And there is almost an arrogance in the way we function in the world. We're not very worried about proving much of anything. Cuban-American literature has a certain swagger. The struggle is different than the Puerto Rican struggle. Cuban-American literature doesn't spend a lot of time asserting its *Cubanness*, it just sort of *is*.

EDR: Let's talk about labels for a moment. How do you see yourself? Are you a Cuban, Cuban-American, Latina?

AO: The fact that I was born in Havana colors everything in my life. If it were not for that fact, everything would be different. The Cuban part of it is fixed, whether I'm a Cuban writer, a Cuban-American writer, or a Cuban who writes. The Cuban thing is the most constant. I think that's because it's the identity that's imposed, and the identity that's most passively available, in the sense that there are specific cultural customs that come from that identity that can't be shaken. That I'm queer is pretty constant, too, but in a different way. My generation didn't grow up queer. You discover it later in life, in adolescence or in adulthood, and then you learn how to be queer. Learning to be Cuban is not a conscious act. You just *are*. You don't get to choose.

EDR: Your latest novel, *Days of Awe*, explores another side of your identity. How did you become interested in the *anusim*?[6]

AO: At the very beginning, through my dad, in a vague sort of way. He was always very knowledgeable about the subject. Then, one day in Boston after a reading, someone asked me if I was Jewish, and I said no. It wasn't like a light bulb turned on over my head or anything, but after that I became more interested in this idea that I had [had] inside me all long. So, I approached my dad and asked him about it, and he downplayed it. He said, "Yeah, there were Jews in our family. They converted a long time ago. It doesn't mean anything." He was really nonchalant. As I started to do research, my work was based not on a literary question but a personal one.

EDR: The book's title refers to the darkest period in the Jewish year, with its focus on sin and atonement.[7] How does that relate to Alejandra's life?

AO: Alejandra judges Enrique rather harshly. She doesn't understand his ambiguity. Because Enrique has lived in a culture where there is no free expression, he has learned to speak in metaphor. He lays out all the clues for Alejandra, but it's really important for her to hear him say out loud, without equivocation, "Yes, I'm a Jew." Of course, he can't do that, and he won't do that. He does everything *but* that, and it takes her a long time to accept the "unspokenness" of things. At the end, she understands, and no longer questions why her father is performing certain Jewish rituals. It's an act of forgiveness towards him. The other larger suggestion, in terms of the book's title, is related to the idea that Cubans judge each other very harshly. There's a lot of judgment between Cubans in terms of [who is] pro- or anti-Castro. For instance, my parents' generation of exiles judges the Marielitos.[8] The people who came on planes judge the people who came on boats. And on and on. If we Cubans plan on having a future, if Cuba has a possibility of a peaceful and prosperous future, we will have to forgive each other.

Ricardo Pau-Llosa

∴ ∴ ∴

Ricardo Pau-Llosa was born in Havana in 1954 and has lived in the United States since 1960. His awards are numerous, and his books of verse include Sorting Metaphors, Bread of the Imagined, *and* Vereda Tropical. Cuba, *the hundredth title in the Carnegie Mellon Poetry Series, was nominated for the 1993 Pulitzer Prize. His 2003 collection,* The Mastery Impulse, *is perhaps his finest work, as it truly captures the poet's ability to express what he himself terms "the Exilic Imagination." In addition to poetry, Pau-Llosa is also well known for his expertise in contemporary Latin American art. He has served as co-curator of two major national exhibits featuring the works of Latino and Latin American artists, as well as authoring several monographs on key Latin American painters.*

Immaculately dressed and holding a fine cigar, Pau-Llosa's appearance is a reflection of his poetry. Or is it vice versa? The smooth and elegant lines of his verse are as carefully crafted as his guayabera. While there is an intensity about the man, especially when he speaks of Cuba, his emotions never impede his thoughtfully conceived responses. His poetry, deeply influenced by phenomenology, reflects this duality, as it focuses on the real and immediate, but only as a springboard for larger, imaginative concepts.

His first published book of poems, Sorting Metaphors, *is a guide to Pau-Llosa's wanderings through the world of the imagination. The title of the book is perhaps a bit misleading, as his images are not simple comparisons intended to evoke an emotional response from his readers. Pau-Llosa's interest, and the strength of his poetry, lies in the intellectual and collective experience exile has helped shape. His subsequent publications reaffirm the poet's disdain of what he considers evocative ethnic literature. In these later works, he focuses instead on the preservation of genuine Cuban art and culture.* Vereda Tropical, *a book dealing with Miami, the city in which he has lived most of his life, is a testament to this.*

As we speak, Pau-Llosa shows me around his Coral Gables home, which is an homage to Cuban and Latin American art. In this interview, conducted on November 10, 2004, Pau-Llosa discusses the creative process and how it relates to phenomenology, his perception of the exile community in Miami, and the role language and memory play in Cuban-American poetry.

Works

Parable Hunter (2008)

The Mastery Impulse (2003)

Vereda Tropical (1999)

The Hollow (1999)

Cuba (1993)

Bread of the Imagined (1992)

Un acercamiento a Polesello (1984)

Sorting Metaphors (1983)

❖

EDR: Let's start by talking about the use of the imagination in your poetry. I've read that if left to your own devices, you would never get out of the city into nature, and that it was your wife who helped you tap in to that other part of your personality. I find that odd since much of your poetry seems to connect to Nature, what is natural, in the Wordsworthian sense.

RPLL: Well, yes, I would like to be a better outdoorsman, but I just don't have those skills. I was never much of an athlete or was never very good at that. Of course, as you suggest with Wordsworth, writers have made nature into much more than the expansive habitat of nonhuman life. Nature is the flowing of the Gods. The Divine is connected to Nature—an idea which has played a role in literature and art for so long that even if you walked outside of your flat in any major city, looking at a tree or crossing a park would suffice to immerse you in Nature as a theme, as a context of the Imagination. Add to that the fact that since the age of six, I grew up in exile and Cuba has always been a real presence in my mind. You get trained spiritually. . . . Exile had already trained me to deal with realities that are distant, or that are foreign, or that are prohibited. I guess the paradox is more pronounced in my case because of the fact that my major philosophical orientation is phenomenology, which is a school of thought very much grounded in the act of perception of the immediate and the consciousness of the moment. So, yes, the vividness of natural images in my work is somewhat of a paradox.

EDR: How does the imagination work in the poetic reconstruction of Cuba?

RPLL: Usually when people talk about the imagination, they talk about it as a faculty that replaces experience. Obviously, that's not how artists see the Imagination. It's a faculty of the mind that can be disciplined in order to make you more in touch with the physical world than the average individual who experiences the world in terms of identifiable things and their functions. Seen phenomenologically, first through suspension and then reconstitution of everyday objects and events, the world becomes vivid and always new. The Imagination is the oxygen of the mind for the artist. It isn't just simply a faculty or a power that can be engaged when you are creating; it has to be turned on all the time. If you don't live in the Imagination and use it to filter every aspect of experience, you will not be able to create anything. It orchestrates the accumulation of experiences and feelings one has garnered simply by living. Imagination, furthermore, links the process of experience and reflection with that of articulation of those experiences, in ways the average person cannot surmise. What happens to many writers who are not profound, or who cultivate an anti-intellectual persona, is that this projection forces them to live in the world in the same way everyone else does. They're not experiencing the world imaginatively at all times, and the result is that often their work is about only one particular thing, or becomes obsessively personal or superficially political, or narrowly focused on matters of the medium itself and technique, gimmicks really. All great art manifests an unexpected vitality, which is possible only as a result of living imaginatively.

EDR: I know you've been influenced by Wallace Stevens.[1] What other writers have had an effect on your work?

RPLL: The list is huge, and the effect is always varied and unexpected. I love the poetry of Derek Walcott for its thoughtful hedonism, its music and images daringly pushed to the limit.[2] Richard Wilbur is another poet who's amazing.[3] Most people read Wilbur and see only his brilliant formalism and sense of structure, the effortless rhymes, et cetera. But Wilbur usually invents a form that suits each poem. I also love the theatricality of the poems. You walk into his work. You feel like you're "in" this space that he has created. He is the master of the poem as habitat and stage at the same time. Rilke is a poet that I read all the time for the same reason.[4] I admire the poets who can give me that enveloping sense, so that, as a reader, I'm still in the world the artist shares with everyone, but the way the whole thing has been constructed has redefined the conditions by which I'm in that shared world. Rilke is the poet-philosopher par excellence, not a mix of the two but both simultaneously.

EDR: I'd like to go back to the role of the Imagination. You said once that Exilic Imagining is a defiance of history, as true creative imagining is a defiance of time. More precisely, Exilic Imagining at the service of creativity unites both defiances.[5] Can you explain and elaborate on this?

RPLL: In poetry, clarity and precision of observation and metaphor represent, for me, a response to the excessive indulgence in the personal as the provider of a poem's emotional force. Perhaps because I had seen so much emotional catharsis in my life growing up, because of Cuba, because of the loss of country, seeing your nation submerged in totalitarianism, seeing your parents dealing with exile and receiving news from Cuba, or going to see people who had just come from Cuba and hearing all these stories, that so-and-so was shot or arrested. . . . These things contained high emotional voltage. For me, this was more cathartic than reading Anne Sexton or Sylvia Plath, poets who seemed obsessed with their own personal anxieties in a narrow sense.[6] I needed something else. I had all that voltage in my life, but it was on an epic scale. For me, the tragedy of Cuba and the aftereffects of that tragedy were transcendent because they weren't personal, although countless real people were being affected. It wasn't about *one* person's psychosis or problems, it was six million people who had decided to embark on this absurd experiment and the toll of death and destruction would be phenomenal. It is when personal suffering becomes collective that it invites a reflection others can benefit from. Witnessing this, and witnessing the witnesses of this, meant that a poetry of just personal expression would be unsatisfactory. That's actually one of the gripes I have with a lot of "ethnic" literature, of whatever ethnicity, that deals with personal adapting or not adapting. . . . I'm someone from Atlantis who has managed to survive, since childhood, the submergence of his culture. I tell people who want to put me in an ethnic box that I am a Minoan-American. Cataclysm has very little to do with the purely personal, with the minutely personal.

EDR: Wouldn't some of these writers argue, though, that in the minutely personal, they find the epic dimension that you speak of?

RPLL: In American culture and American life, there is one fundamental difference in context that differs from my own particular sense of cultural space. I had a cataclysmic sense of that space. I saw my culture annihilated. Americans still don't have that. Americans float in a landscape that has no sense of that. No sense of termination. They can be thankful for that but not pretend they know it.

EDR: Why do you think some other writers don't have the same sense of the epic proportions of the Cuban condition?

RPLL: It may have to do with the fact that we—my family and I—didn't come to Miami until I was fourteen. So, the contrast between Cuba post-1959 and America as this boundless terrain may have been augmented by the fact that we went to Chicago and then to Tampa. Tampa in the '60s was a typical immigrant city in that, for many Cuban exiles, their culture was a distant reference, a thing in the past. These recent arrivals from Cuba absorbed this immigrant mindset from third-generation Americans of Spanish, Italian, and Cuban descent. For me, Cuba was a very defined, real thing that perished. Also, I came from very working-class parents. For me, Cuba wasn't the lost palace, like, for example, [it is for] Carlos Eire.[7] That's also the kind of excessive personal nostalgia that I didn't want. It wasn't for me about the privileged life I would have had if there had not been this so-called revolution. I wasn't a member of that class. I may not be giving you the clear answer you want. I was, from the age of six to fourteen, surrounded by the American immigrant experience, while configuring Cuba as a lost landscape, not as a lost heirloom.

EDR: Despite this contrast that you just mentioned, in your poetry, there is no sense of the duality, the inner conflict, that is the staple of other ethnic writers.

RPLL: Let's take Husserl.[8] For Husserl, you have to put aside, to bracket, the things that are not part of the immanent experience, that are culturally acquired connotations of something. So, for a lot of writers, or Cubans, in general, Cuba was already tinged with all this nostalgia. As someone influenced by phenomenology, I had to bracket that. For me, the question was: What am I actually looking at when I look at Cuban art, or my own Cuban memories and experiences? What is immanent comes first, so that you first arrive at the phenomenologically vivid perception of the presence of this image or recollection in Being. Let's take this coffee cup. You don't know who made it. Any cultural connection to a coffee cup is not immanent. What's immanent is the shape, the form, the shine, whatever. Then you understand that as the ground on upon which you reconstitute the fact that it is a cup, because even its function has to be bracketed. So you rebuild from the ground up, from the ground of sensorial experience. If you do that, nostalgia appears as this sentimental complicity in loss. That doesn't even come in, because that is such a peripheral aspect of that which you have already decided to focus on and ground your perception on. What comes into the act of the mind before the nostalgia is the history, the actual causes and effects that led to this coffee cup being here. And then, eighteen dimensions later, come your emotional responses to the cup.

EDR: What role does memory play in this equation?

RPLL: Memory is very important because first comes the immanent, then the historical causes, then little by little you introduce your own personal element. So, what phenomenology taught me was a discipline by which I could deal with these things as an artist, and see where emotions belong, but not at the center of it—or not always at the center. Whereas someone who is not interested in this kind of rigor might see the coffee cup and think, "Oh, my tía [aunt] used to make coffee and pour it in a cup just like this one," and so the poem becomes about tía, or about abuela's [grandmother's], coffee cup. They don't allow themselves to become interested in these other foundational structures first. As an artist, these are very important to me, and I think that one of the reasons they are important is the influence of the visual arts on me. A painting cannot afford to be as loose with these emotional responses to memory. A painter cannot afford to be "mugged" by his own emotions.

EDR: How did phenomenology influence your first book of poetry, *Sorting Metaphors*?

RPLL: One of the things I became interested in was metaphor as such because, while Husserl was interested in the perception of things, I also understood that a poet is somebody working with language and with chains of words, and with meaning created out of chains of words, that have an arc, and have a conclusion, and all these linguistic aspects. You also, then, have this thing called language, which is also part of the phenomenological experience. Creatively you have to deal with language in an equally rigorous manner. The language poets use has an almost chaotic, atomic, interaction of concepts of words. Language constructs meaning in ways totally differently from the way we constitute the identity and function of things in the world. Hence, applying the phenomenological suspension to language would take on different aspects than applying it to things in the world, even different from its application to images in memory. I understood I would be dealing with these two, perhaps incompatible, structures of thought. So, one of the things I did was start working with poems that tried to avoid syntax. How can I use the encounter with the thing, and how can I use metaphor to align itself with that pursuit of phenomenological immanence first? I wrote a series of poems in that book [*Sorting Metaphors*] that are metaphor sequences. "Red Hole," for instance, is like a ladder of metaphors that ends with the triggering referent: the harvest moon. The idea was to use metaphor as the poet's instrument for engaging in writing the phenomenological *epoche*, because after all when you're writing a poem, it's not the same as when you're looking at this coffee cup. You have the object in front of you, but when you're writing a poem, you have to think that there's a reader, and not only of words. When my parents were talking about Cuba, I was being bombarded with these images of the lost country. Dealing with intersubjectivity—the way others represent and then articulate their feelings and memories—had to become, I thought, part of the essential—non-bracketable—experience of the poem. Or was it essential? I wanted to create a state of consciousness that was like mine when I was looking at something, so by eliminating the syntax, I was hoping to achieve that. Every line has to be charged, because I'm not interested in *talking* to you; you've got to walk into my room, and the room is going to hit you with stimuli. Just by sitting here, if you sit in my house, you can see that my rooms are filled with stimuli anyway.

EDR: As I look around your home, I can't help but connect the space that you create in your poems with the one you've created here. How did you first become interested in painting, and how does that interest inform your poetry?

RPLL: For me painting is so important because it has that carnality of the moment. That sense of the image imposing itself and blocking out everything else. The painting is the universe, and the universe starts at the frame and goes in. A work of art is egomaniacal in that it demands surrender; it sucks you in. Paintings that are good have that capacity, and they also taught me how to look at the world, because obviously, even the most abstract and non-referential painter is gleaning something from the world. On a more personal level, painting also allowed me to connect to the Latin American experience. For me, the work of art was a very tangible, palpable presence of a culture, in a way that the recollections or accounts of somebody or memories about Cuba [were] not. When you fill a space, as I have my house, with paintings and sculptures, it is not out of *horror vacui* but out of a lust for simultaneity, a lust for the velocity of which the imagination alone is capable.

EDR: As you know, there is a strong relationship between phenomenology and existentialism. One of the tenets of existentialism is the necessity of choice. You have chosen to "set the record straight" when it comes to Cuba. Do you see that as an obligation?

RPLL: Yes. It comes from an existentialist obligation when you're in an environment where everyone thinks that Cuba before 1959 was the same thing as Honduras or Haiti or some backward place. Not that there's anything wrong with Honduras or Haiti, but that wasn't Cuba. Was it an advanced, developed nation? No. But it wasn't this backward nation, either. Americans, especially, look at things in terms of preconceived patterns. They can't look at Cuba as a police state, a reality you are obligated to denounce precisely because you're a liberal. They hear buzz words like "socialism" or "equality," and that's enough for them to set aside skepticism and not see what it really is. They yearn for an ideological Disney World, and the Cuban regime uses that yearning to entice them. What I don't understand about American political life is that the people who are supposed to be on the side of the Cuban exiles and the Cuban dissidents fighting Castro are the ones who are on the side of Castro. American Democrat politicians, like Maxine Waters or Christopher Dodd, go to Cuba, and they don't see that it's an all-white government oppressing a country that's 75 percent black? They don't see that there are no independent trade unions, and yet, they are Democrats and liberals who are supposed to be very interested in trade unions. I don't get that. And I think they do get it, but they refuse to see it, for whatever reason. I don't think stupidity or blindness is an adequate excuse in this regard. I have to hold them accountable. There are principles they are betraying—their own alleged principles.

EDR: I read a quote by Jonathan Kandell where he calls you "the rarest of specimens" because you are a conservative poet.[9] He seems to think that all artists are, or should be, liberal. Can you comment on this?

RPLL: Yes, that's right, "the rarest of specimens." Kandell is a former writer for *The New York Times*. He grew up in Mexico and speaks Spanish fluently. He was sent down here to do a feature on Miami for *Cigar Aficionado*. It's very curious that all these people who are advocating the end of the American embargo never bring up this other dichotomy. Everywhere in the world, business is considered bad from a radical perspective, except in Cuba. That's the only place it's considered good. Why? If Cuba has no American business, it has no American exploitation, so it should be a floating island of wondrous prosperity. According to them, American businesses are ruthless, vicious vampires, so it follows that in Cuba, where there is no American business, it should be great. No! They claim that Cuba is the exception. There, we must have American business. Actually, these liberals routinely engage in flagrant illogic. They claim American tourism and trade would advance democracy in Cuba, and then say if we trade with other tyrannies—China, Saudi Arabia—why not trade with Cuba? Well, you can't have both: it's either trade democratizes or it has no effect on democracy, and we shouldn't care, either, business is business. What poor opinion these liberals have of other people's intelligence. Betty Friedan, to my face, told me, at the opening of an art fair in Miami in January 1999, after she had returned from Cuba after being there for a month, that it was a "pity that we, Americans, didn't allow that socialist experiment to work."[10] Here is a feminist icon who had just come from an island where women are brutally exploited sexually by foreigners, where prostitution is the only private enterprise allowed by the police state, so that the state becomes the pimp-in-chief, and her response was *we* Americans have not allowed this social experiment to work! What am I supposed to read from this garbage?! Where are your wonderful liberal credentials and perceptions and analyses on the subtext of oppression? In any other western setting that is not Communist, all that gets dismantled, hacked away, but there [in Cuba], it's a whole other different reality for these people. That is lunacy. That is complicity with a police state.

EDR: Let's switch from Havana to your present home. *Vereda Tropical* is about Miami, which you call "Thing City." Not a flattering depiction. Can you explain what you were trying to do there?

RPLL: One of the fundamental tasks of exile is to preserve cultural continuity. The failure of the exile community to really understand themselves as exiles—they chant exile, they call themselves exiles, but they don't act like exiles. Part of what exiles are supposed to do is to preserve their culture. Look at the model of the Jewish diaspora. There is a preservation of a culture that is astonishing. It's a great human epic told and immortalized and therefore cherished by Jews and non-Jews alike. Cubans don't do that. Cubans in less than two generations have completely abandoned their own culture. They extol their economic and political successes without grasping how, given these successes, their failure to preserve their culture through institutions and the like becomes all the more damning because of their success.

EDR: When you say culture, you don't mean black beans and a guayabera.

RPLL: Of course not. There is no Cuban museum! I had this experience: A French official had arrived in Miami and contacted me because, at the time, I was the senior editor for *Art International* in the United States, which was a Paris-based magazine, and he wanted me to show him the museums et cetera. He wanted me to show him "Cuba in exile." I had to take him to the houses of artists to see their work! I couldn't take this man to a Cuban museum! Here we have a million Cuban exiles from every stratum of Cuban society, including major artists and writers, and we don't have a single cultural institution that is run by Cubans! There are Mexican museums in California and Texas, there are Jewish museums everywhere. . . . Every group has its ethnic institution in its own hands; at least, they have a showcase of their culture. We don't have that. We can't be bothered with culture; we loathe the future because, from ignorance, we are embarrassed by the phony past we've been told is ours.

EDR: Is this the failure that you are trying to describe in *Vereda Tropical*?

RPLL: In *Vereda Tropical*, I was interested in the performance of Cuban music. In May 1995, there opened in Miami a place called Café Nostalgia. It was a small cabaret, featuring Cuban music live, *descargas*,[11] from top-notch brilliant musicians. It also played, between sets, vintage videos of Cuban music from the golden age of the '40s and '50s. I was there every night. I was seeing Cuban culture alive and evolving, the same escape from Cuba-as-death I had experienced in the exile art scene twenty years earlier. I was there every night with my pad. The poems of *Vereda Tropical* were written there, mostly. But then the musicians were replaced by others who weren't quite as good. The magic lasted for about six months. My parents would go to cabarets in Cuba practically every night, and they would see La Lupe, and Elena Burque, and Benny Moré, all the time.[12] These same people, exiles, come here, and they start a city, and their music is left to flounder. Anywhere you go in the world, there is Cuban music. And in Miami, I can't hear live, new, evolving Cuban music. This is outrageous! Of course, I condemn Miami. The Haitians have done more with their own culture in Miami, in far less time and with far fewer resources. The Nicaraguans have done more. Thirty or 40 percent of exhibitions in the Miami Art Museum in downtown Miami should be Cuban, another 20 or 30 percent should be Latin American, and maybe 20 percent, something else. But Cubans exert no pressure on the existing cultural institutions here, and they don't start their own either. Even the music, the most accessible art form and the one everyone admits we excelled in and still do, is left to its own pathetic devices. I mean, the profound, original music that deepened and diversified the *son* and bolero and rumba and cha-cha, not the ephemeral dance and pop stuff.

EDR: Let's talk about your latest book of poems, *Mastery Impulse*. What is the significance of the title?

RPLL: It comes from Freud, from one of his early essays, titled "Infantile Sexuality," where he writes that the sexual impulse is connected to mastery, and he uses that phrase in passing, "mastery impulse." I play with that phrase partly in the Freudian sense, but also in the sense of mastering reality, and using the imagination to master the chaos of experiences. So, the book is broken up into different versions of how one masters these things that emerge, from everyday objects in the first part of the book, to things that deal with sexuality, to things that deal with history. I also deal with parables, with parables as the triumph of the imagination over the flux, of the phenomenological and existential theme. I'm not actually interested in creating parables, but in that *impulse* of creating parables. That is the focus of my new book, in process [*Parable Hunter*].

EDR: Finally, let me ask you about language. Do you think that English is a necessary part of the exilic imagination?

RPLL: I don't. I think you can write in Spanish, or in French, or whatever. For me, though, English was and is essential. I was raised here and educated in American schools. I practically lost my Spanish. Now, I am fluent in both, but English allowed me, and still does, a flexibility and a sense of ambiguity, which Spanish doesn't. I'm writing in English because I was brought up in the United States. It's one of my two native languages. The training of my imagination was in English.

Gustavo Pérez Firmat

⁘ ⁘ ⁘

*Author and literary critic Gustavo Pérez Firmat was born in Cuba in 1949
and immigrated to the United States in 1960. He lives in Chapel Hill,
North Carolina, where he taught in Duke University's Department of
Modern Languages from 1978 to 1999. Pérez Firmat has been the recipi-
ent of fellowships from the National Endowment for the Humanities, the
American Council of Learned Societies, and the Guggenheim Foundation.
In 1997,* Newsweek *included him among "100 Americans to watch for in
the next century," and* Hispanic Business Magazine *selected him as one of
the "100 most influential Hispanics." He is currently the David Feinson
Professor of Humanities at Columbia University in New York City.*

*Pérez Firmat's work has had a profound impact on Cuban-American
studies. His many nonfiction publications include* Literature and Liminality: Festive Readings in the Hispanic Tradition *(1986);* The Cuban
Condition: Translation and Identity in Modern Cuban Literature *(1989);
and* Life on the Hyphen: The Cuban-American Way *(1994). He has also
published four poetry collections, a novel, and most recently a memoir,*
Scar Tissue *(2005), chronicling his bout with prostate cancer.*

Life on the Hyphen *is perhaps his most significant work, as it has
helped guide the direction of Cuban-American literary studies. In it, Pérez
Firmat builds on sociologist Rubén Rumbaut's labeling of children who
were born abroad but educated and raised in the United States as the*

one-and-a-half generation. *Pérez Firmat applies the term to Cuban-born writers, such as himself, who left the island at an early age and were raised in the United States. In contrast to Rumbaut, Pérez Firmat focuses on this generation to emphasize its simultaneous adaptability to both cultures. He sees the members of this generation living* within *the hyphen, able to navigate either world with linguistic and cultural ease. Pérez Firmat's wit and intense interest in linguistic nuances is best revealed in his poetry, where often the speaker is living life "on the hyphen," grappling with the ambivalence of belonging to two seemingly disparate worlds.*

As I park in the driveway of his home in Chapel Hill, Pérez Firmat appears, dressed in shorts and a tee-shirt, having just returned from the gym. This energy and vitality, which echoes in his work, is evident during our conversation. His penchant for linguistic play is ever present, even when discussing such somber topics as cancer and the death of his father. The date is June 20, 2006.

Works

Scar Tissue (2005)

Tongue Ties: Logo-Eroticism in Anglo-Hispanic Literature (2003)

Cincuenta lecciones de exilio y desexilio (2000)

Anything But Love (2000)

Vidas en vilo: La cultura cubanoamericana (2000)

My Own Private Cuba: Essays on Cuban Literature and Culture (1999)

Next Year in Cuba (1995)

Bilingual Blues (1995)

Life on the Hyphen: The Cuban-American Way (1994)

Do the Americans Have a Common Literature? (editor, 1990)

Equivocaciones (1989)

The Cuban Condition: Translation and Identity in Modern Cuban Literature (1989)

"Carolina Cuban" (in *Triple Crown*, 1987)

Literature and Liminality: Festive Readings in the Hispanic Tradition (1986)

Idle Fictions: The Hispanic Vanguard Novel, 1926–1934 (1982)

∴

EDR: I'd like to start with your most recent effort, *Scar Tissue*. What made you want, or need, to write about your experience with cancer?

GPF: A couple of years ago, two things happened that changed my life, were my life changeable: my father passed away in Miami after waiting for forty years to return to some mysterious place he called Cuba, and I was diagnosed with prostate cancer, a disease that he also had. Because the two events occurred within a couple of months of each other, they bundled together in my mind and out came *Scar Tissue*, a sickly, sticky sequel to *Next Year in Cuba* and *Life on the Hyphen*, where I write about enduring illness in a foreign language, about coping with losses of various sorts (*de padre, de patria y de próstata*),[1] and generally about the hurt inside the hyphen. (It turns out that the hyphen was a scar all along!) In *Scar Tissue*—my informal title is "Knife on the Hyphen"—I write about prostate cancer, a common but unliterary disease, with the same candor and even ardor with which others have written about breast cancer or AIDS. Kafka says somewhere that a book should be the axe for the frozen sea inside us. After the surgeons took a scalpel to my belly, I took an axe to my *entrañas*.[2] What was left was *Scar Tissue*.

EDR: The final chapter of the book is titled "Beginning." Is this, ironically, a hopeful "fresh start"? If so, how does this sense of wholeness relate to the "confused" state of exile?

GPF: Yes, the last poem in *Scar Tissue* is called "Beginning," but the epilogue is called "Sutures." I don't believe in fresh starts. All fresh starts are really stale starts, and exile is the stalest start of all.

EDR: Your informal title, "Knife on the Hyphen," is an example of the linguistic wordplay your writing often contains. How did you manage to fuse your sense of play into this serious topic?

GPF: Well, *Scar Tissue* includes a manic medical glossary with definitions of such terms as "prostatic" (likes noise; doesn't like motion), "retropubic" (old fashioned pubic); "abdominal surgery" (gut wrenching); "X-ray" (king has-been), "incontinent" (where you are / when you are / not in Cuba), etc. Other parts, however, are dead serious (as it were). When I was recovering from what was, or could have been, or might still be a life-threatening illness, I went through many moods, from high anxiety to deep euphoria. *Scar Tissue* reflects that. Emotionally, the book is all over the place. It's a moods dictionary.

EDR: Can you speak to your use of this type of wordplay in your work in general.

GPF: I like words. I like sentences. If you like something, you spend time with it. If you spend time with it, you get to know it. If you get to know it, it tells you little secrets. I don't make an effort to play with words. Sometimes I make an effort *not* to play with words, because when I'm playing with words I have the sneaking suspicion that the words are actually playing with me. But manipulating language is pleasurable, and it offers me a kind of release. No matter what I'm writing, I tend to write by ear. You come up with a phrase or a sentence that sounds good, and then you realize that it also conveys what you wanted to say—that what sounds good also rings true—or that it conveys something different but perhaps just as pertinent as what you wanted to say. Sense then follows sound. I'm hopelessly, helplessly phonocentric, perhaps because I come from a country where all the men sooner or later go deaf (while the women, on the other hand, get louder and louder, so that their deaf husbands can hear them).

EDR: Clearly, this sense of play often results in humor or is driven by it. Sometimes humor is satiric, such as the way Roberto Fernández[3] pokes fun at Cuban-American nostalgia. How would you characterize the nature and purpose of *your* use of humor?

GPF: I love Roberto's work because beneath the satire, there is a tremendous amount of affection. His novels make fun of Cuban Miami, but they also render homage to it. My humor is ill humor. It grows out of an unstable compound of anger and distress. I'm like a man flailing away in his sleep. He doesn't know what he is flailing at, but he keeps flailing. Wake him up and he doesn't remember flailing, but the next time he goes to sleep, he begins flailing all over again.

EDR: Is your penchant for linguistic play influenced by someone or something in particular?

GPF: Wordplay is much more frequent than one would think because it encompasses a lot more than wordplay. It includes phrase- and sentence- and paragraph-play. Ultimately, it's language-play, which is the same as language use. Take Nabokov's statement: "I'm as American as April in Arizona."[4] What is it about this sentence that makes it memorable? First, it's a variation on "as American as apple pie," a variation made pointed by the near homophony of "apple" and "April." Second, there's the alliteration of American/April/Arizona. Third, and best of all, "Arizona" is not even an "American" word because it sounds Spanish—a compound put together from "zona árida"—but apparently is of Amerindian origin. So is this wordplay? To me it's just a good sentence: cunning rather than punning.

EDR: Why do you find it easier to use this type of play in English than in Spanish?

GPF: For one thing, Spanish has no homophones. For another—and this is the opposite phenomenon—it also has no "homographs." As Ricky Ricardo once pointed out, in Spanish, words that look the same sound the same, and words that sound the same look the same. In English, as he explains, "bough," "cough" and "through" look the same but sound different; and "bough" and "cow" look different but sound the same. Ricky's conclusion: "Crazy language!" The other reason may be personal. Perhaps I feel freer to fool around in, and with, English because it's not my mother or father's tongue. I don't mind writing English with an accent, but I work hard not to write Spanish with an accent. And yet in *Cincuenta lecciones de exilio y desexilio*, which is all in Spanish, there's a fair amount of what might be regarded as wordplay.

EDR: Do you believe that English is a necessary component of Cuban-American literature? There are members of the one-and-a-half generation[5] who write mostly in English. Others, like Roberto Fernández, have produced more in Spanish than English. Should they not be included in an anthology of Cuban-American literature?

GPF: Yes, of course. It would be interesting to put together an anthology of Cuban-American (or, for that matter, Latino) literature that does not discriminate between anglophone and hispanophone writing. Or an anthology of one writer, say Roberto Fernández, who writes in both languages: the Roberto Reader, which would mix selections in Spanish and English. The problem is [that] even publishers who publish in both languages tend not to want to mix them within the same book. I wonder, though, what makes a novel written in Spanish by Roberto Fernández "Cuban American" rather than "Cuban." A Mariel writer like Guillermo Rosales,[6] who in *Boarding Home* wrote in Spanish about his experiences in the United States, is usually not considered Cuban-American. However, José Miguel Oviedo,[7] in his history of Spanish American literature, says that Oscar Hijuelos,[8] whom I regard as an American ethnic writer, is the first Cuban writer to write exclusively in English.

The relation between language and nationality is tricky. And it's a mistake to identify literary nationality with civil nationality. Even though George Santayana[9] was not American, he said: "It is as an American writer that I am to be counted, if I'm to be counted at all." So, here was a Spanish man who was an American writer; just as Conrad[10] was a Polish man who was an English novelist. As you know, my definition of a Cuban-American is a Cuban married to an American, and my definition of a Cuban-American writer is a Cuban who writes in English. And so I don't think of myself as a Cuban or American or Cuban-American writer, but rather as a Cuban who sometimes writes in English and, at other times, writes in Spanish. And it's always the language I'm not writing that is my home. I can't write in English without missing the Spanish that is missing. I can't write in Spanish without missing the English that is missing. These are the sorts of "tongue ties" I've tried to unravel in a recent book.

About the use of Spanish in Cuban-American literature: I think you'll agree that most one-and-a-halfers write mostly in English, for both practical and existential reasons. In fact, Latino literature has become an English-only zone. The use of Spanish in Latino fiction or poetry tends to be ornamental, a dash of spice or *un brochazo* [a brushstroke] of local color.

EDR: Since we're talking about other writers, are there any, particularly Cuban ones, that influenced you?

GPF: Since I teach literature, I have to read for my classes, and some of the literature that I teach finds its way into what I write, even if I'm not aware of it. A few years ago I published a novel called *Anything But Love*. Some time later, I was teaching *El túnel*, a book by Ernesto Sábato, that I had taught many times before, and was surprised by all the echoes of *Anything But Love* in *El túnel* (actually the other way around). But I'm not really an avid reader. Growing up in Miami—a boutique rather than a book city—I read hardly at all. The nuns in the parochial school I attended used to punish me by making me come in on Saturday mornings to read. I had to sit in the library for two hours. But the only thing I remember reading was a biography of American patriot John Paul Jones. Some of the writers whose work I have admired, envied, and (perhaps) learned from throughout the years: Jorge Mañach,[11] John Updike, A. E. Housman, Borges,[12] Jane Austen, Scott Fitzgerald, Lezama Lima,[13] Cabrera Infante[14] (the nonfiction more than the fiction), Alejandra Pizarnik,[15] Christopher Morley (the Mandarin poems), Henry James (the novellas), Roberto Fernández, Virgil Suárez. As I recite the names that pop into my head, I realize what an arbitrary, chaotic list this is. Even more chaotic if you add the nonliterary influences: American song lyricists from the 1930s and 1940s; Cuban and American comedians, like

Leopoldo Fernández, Guillermo Álvarez Guedes, Henny Youngman, Alan King; and many other people I remember and don't remember. I'm the sum total of my influences—plus the 5 percent that belongs only to me.

EDR: Let's talk a bit about your childhood. You left Cuba at eleven years old. Can you talk a bit about your early life in the U.S., and what that process of assimilation, or "biculturation" as you've called it, was like.

GPF: I came to the U.S. when I was on the cusp of adolescence. I have fuzzy fond memories of Cuba and sharp fond memories of our early years in Miami. Cuba seemed so close then. The only people in my family who weren't alive were those who hadn't been born yet. Now things are different. Most of the people in my family who are still alive are those who hadn't been born when we came to the United States. And Cuba seems far, far away. To the extent that assimilation happened, it happened imperceptibly and had already begun even before we came to the United States. As I mention in *Next Year in Cuba*, I was raised for exile: I learned English in grade school, watched American movies, ate American breakfasts, rode around in American cars, rooted for the New York Yankees. American culture was foreign but familiar, and even familial, since my mother was born in Norfolk, Virginia, when my grandfather was a member of the Cuban consulate there. And yet, although America is a part of me, it's not the most important part of me. No matter how assimilated I may act or look, there is always an unassimilable remainder, a Cuban core, which only seems to get larger with the years.

EDR: How does memory, especially memories of Cuba, shape your work, and the work of other Cuban-American writers?

GPF: In younger writers, Ana Menéndez[16] or Richard Blanco,[17] for example, memories of Cuba tend to be reported rather than remembered. They are something they write about rather than something they write with. Even Virgil Suárez or Roberto Fernández or Ricardo Pau-Llosa,[18] who are somewhat older, write to some extent about the second-handedness of their memories. As for me, when I grow nostalgic, it's not for the Havana of my childhood, but for the Miami of my adolescence. Still, I do feel some sort of responsibility—more as a father than as a writer—not to let my children forget their grandparents and great-grandparents and other Cuban relatives, and I take it upon myself to perpetuate their stories, which are the stories of Cuba. It's a responsibility that I'm not crazy about. A couple of years ago, during our

Nochebuena[19] celebration, I realized that I was the oldest Cuban in the house. This sent me into a depression that hasn't quite lifted yet.

EDR: Another component of Cuban-American literature is exile. Would you say it's the key component?

GPF: I don't know whether it's the key component, but it's certainly a component. It explains something you mentioned before: why Cuban-American writers still write in Spanish, even though some of them have lived here for more than forty years. But what I find most peculiar is exile literature written in English that pines for the homeland in a language that makes that homeland more distant. Longing for Cuba in the language of Cuba makes sense; longing for Cuba in the language of America is a little strange, and yet I and others do it all the time. Odder still, often the nostalgia is directed at the Spanish language itself. This longing for Spanish in English is one of the features that Cuban-American literature has in common with Puerto Rican or Chicano literature. Latino literature, whatever its ethnicity, is full of English-language love songs to Spanish, love songs that happen also to be valedictories. The Latino writer carries a torch he or she can't lose for Spanish, the language she or he has lost. Sandra Cisneros has a poem that begins, "Make love to me in Spanish, / not with that other tongue."[20] Okay, fine, but if we both know Spanish, why are you telling me this in English?

EDR: Because of your wordplay, you've been compared to the Metaphysical Poets.[21] One of the things the Metaphysicals did was juxtapose the sacred and the profane. Your poem "A Sensitive Male's Mea Culpa" is perhaps an extreme version of this. What sort of reaction did you receive to this poem and others, such as "The Poet Discusseth the Opposite Sex"?

GPF: The poems you mention, and especially "A Sensitive Male's Mea Culpa," seem to me a lot more physical than metaphysical. When I wrote "Mea Culpa," I sent it to a friend, who wrote back: "Never publish this!!" So, of course, I went ahead and published it. Unlike "Bilingual Blues" or "Dedication or Lime Cure," it's not one of the poems that people bring up. I think it makes some people queasy, though to me it's a very funny poem. I wrote it in a huff sometime during the heyday of the political correctness movement. Your reference to the Metaphysical Poets embarrasses me. Comparing me to Crashaw is like comparing a weekend golfer with a thirty handicap to Tiger Woods.

EDR: Perhaps, but many of your poems reveal a certain melancholy. They are spoken by a sinner who seems to be searching for something. What?

GPF: I agree about the melancholy, but I don't think of myself as a sinner. In fact, I haven't sinned since I left Cuba. When I got on the boat to leave, God said: "Go, and sin no more." And I haven't. Even if I have, though, I'm not worried. When I was in Catholic school, we learned that each prayer entitled you to a certain number of days off in purgatory. These things were called indulgences. The best prayers were those that granted you *indulgencia plenaria*, plenary indulgence, which meant that you wouldn't have to spend any time at all paying for your sins. In my view, all exiles are entitled to plenary indulgence. One more thing: In English, a small sin is a peccadillo, but to a Cuban this sounds like something you eat.[22]

EDR: Obviously your nonfiction is highly personal and grounded in real events. Do you feel that poetry should also be grounded on what is real and personal?

GPF: What I know is that I have a hard time inventing anything, at least on purpose, whether I'm writing poetry or prose. I do have a need, which to me is as natural as breathing, to write things down—whether formally, in a book or a poem, or informally, in my journals. Sometimes I write things down to remember them. Other times I write them down to forget them. The personal quality of all my work is obviously a limitation, but I discovered years ago that I couldn't keep myself out of what I wrote, and so I stopped trying.

EDR: Earlier you mentioned your novel, *Anything But Love*. That book shifts between points of view and, at times, seems autobiographical. Do you consider it a work of fiction or a memoir, much like *Scar Tissue*?

GPF: Sometimes I think that I should have written it all in the first person, but at the time, I was afraid that Frank's ranting would become tiresome. And so, in the middle section, I switched to the third person to create some distance (between him and me, between the reader and him). The nucleus of the novel was originally a chapter in *Next Year in Cuba* that my publisher refused to include in the book, believing it would hurt sales. So, I decided to turn it into an independent story, which allowed me to take liberties with the narrative and give it a shape that it wouldn't otherwise have had. So, yes, it's somewhere between memoir and novel.

EDR: What was the reaction from those who know you best, like your family, to some of the things you wrote in *Next Year in Cuba*? Did this affect your decision to make *Anything But Love* into a novel?

GPF: I can't recall very many nice things that my family said about *Next Year in Cuba*. I was hoping they'd be impressed and even flattered, but mostly they were upset that I had aired out our dirty laundry in public. It may also be the case that the man who wrote that book was not the son or brother or cousin that they knew. My mother, in particular, was very angry with the chapter about my father, even though I wrote it, or I thought I wrote it, not to settle scores but out of love and sorrow. I've never felt closer to my father than when I was writing *Next Year in Cuba*—after all, it's his title. But after my mother's reaction to this book, I stopped giving her copies of some of the things I publish. And so I've never given her *Anything But Love*, or *Scar Tissue*, or a story called "Mami's Boy," which is a kind of act of contrition dedicated to her . . . uhm . . . maybe I am a sinner after all . . .

EDR: You mentioned earlier your humor is often a result of anger and distress. This [*Anything But Love*] seems angrier than your other works. Where did the anger come from?

GPF: This is one of those books that I wrote to forget. It grew out of an especially unhappy time in my life, when I was upset at stuff that had happened to me, or that I thought had happened to me. But the thing about the story is that Frank never does find out the truth about Catherine's past. It's all surmises, theories, inferences on his part. Sometimes the people we know best are the same ones we know least.

EDR: In addition to being a creator of Cuban-American literature, you're also one of its foremost critics. Are you a writer first and critic second?

GPF: I see myself not as a writer but as someone who writes. I write for a variety of reasons: it's my job; it allows me to remember and to forget; and I enjoy it—especially after it's done. I also find that writing criticism is more difficult than writing "creatively," because the range of allowable utterances is narrower. One of the things I've tried to do in my scholarship is stretch the boundaries a little, see how much I can get away with. And so a book like *Life on the Hyphen*, which is scholarship, includes autobiographical vignettes and ends with a poem.

EDR: Do you have any predictions about Cuba once it is free of Castro? Will you ever return?

GPF: My prediction: Whatever happens in Cuba, it will have happened too late. If you were thirty when Castro took over, you are now in your seventies. And if you were older than thirty, you are probably dead. The generation of exiles to whom return would have been truly meaningful is filling up the cemeteries in Miami and elsewhere. This is very sad. Much of the "scar tissue" I carry inside me has little to do with anything that has happened to me, but with what happened to those older exiles who premised their lives in exile on a return that never took place. I wish I could make it up to them. Since I can't, I write poems and stories about my wish to make it up to them.

I haven't gone back to Cuba, and perhaps I never will. Before I didn't go because my father was still alive, and now I don't go because he is not. What's the point of returning if he can't accompany me? Years ago my father would ask whether I would go back to Cuba with him when Castro was gone. I always replied that I would, not knowing whether I really meant it. Now, I ask myself whether I would go back without him, and I don't know what to answer.

Dolores Prida

❖ ❖ ❖

When you meet Dolores Prida, it is hard to believe that this diminutive woman has accomplished so much in her lifetime. The moment she speaks, however, her enthusiasm and humor leave no doubt that she is indeed the author of many award-winning plays. Her home in Spanish Harlem in New York City is as colorful as its resident. As we talk, sipping Cuban coffee, Prida smokes continuously, and her energy is contagious. From her humble beginnings in a small Cuban fishing village, her life has been marked by a series of literary and professional accomplishments.

Prida was born in Caibarién, Cuba, in 1943. She immigrated to the United States in 1961 and studied at Hunter College in New York City. She has worked as an editor for both Spanish- and English-language periodicals, published two volumes of poetry, written documentary films and a screenplay, and seen seven of her plays produced on stage. She has received local, national, and international prizes, including the Cintas Fellowship Award for Literature in 1976. She has also been active in the Cuban-American community, traveling to Cuba and lobbying for the release of political prisoners there.

The thematic content of her plays reveals her desire to correct the double stigmatization to which Hispanic women are subjected. Beautiful Señoritas, for example, satirically condemns beauty pageants while also commenting on traditional chauvinistic rituals. As the little girl at the play's center holds the plot together, the stereotyping of Latina women is developed. Using music, the play's comedic exterior ultimately reveals a serious issue: a woman's quest for self-identity and self-discovery. Coser y Cantar *(Sewing and Singing) is another example of Prida's interest in women's issues. The play depicts two divergent personalities of a female Cuban immigrant debating the pros and cons of Hispanic heritage versus American influence. Initially, there appear to be two separate characters, Ella and She, but it quickly becomes clear that "Her" and "She" are Prida's symbolic representation of a bilingual, bicultural Cuban-American.*

During this conversation on July 6, 2004, Prida discussed her work, her life in and outside of Cuba, and her views on such issues as labeling, gender roles, and language. As her plays' characters do, she often switches between languages when speaking. To preserve the flavor of the original, I have retained her comments in Spanish with my translations immediately following them.

Works

Four Guys Named José and Una Mujer Named María (2000)

Casa Propia (1999)

Hola Olá (1996)

Allentales (1994)

Botánica (1990)

Pantallas (1986)

Savings (1985)

Juan Boob (1981)

Crisp! (1981)

Coser y Cantar (1981)

La Era Latina (1980)

The Beggar's Soap Opera (1979)

Beautiful Señoritas (1977)

∴

EDR: Since we're here in your home, perhaps we should start by talking about your latest play, *Casa Propia* (One's Own Home).

DP: Well, it was inspired by this house. Es una pareja cubana. El personaje principal es Olga. (It's about a Cuban couple. The main character is Olga.) Middle-aged. Su marido, que es un mujeriego, una hija de veintetantos años, y la suegra, la madre de él, que los hijos la trajeron de Cuba como tantos viejos y nadie la quiera, así que los hijos la mandaron para Nueva York. (Her husband, who's a womanizer; a twenty-something daughter; and the mother-in-law—his mother—whose children brought her from Cuba, like happened with so many older Cubans. Nobody wanted her, so the kids sent her to New York.) Olga's husband doesn't want her to have a house because he moves from place to place. He's a traveling salesman. In her monologue, Olga says that the only house she's ever had is a dollhouse that she could fold up and take with her. When she left Cuba, she had to leave it behind. So Olga wants to buy a house.

EDR: How about the house you left behind in Cuba?

DP: I had a very happy childhood. Caibarién is a small fishing town famous for its seafood. So I grew up on the beach.

EDR: And your family? Anything like that of the play?

DP: No. I'm the oldest of three sisters. One of my sisters lives here with me. My mother passed away in '84. My father is about ninety now. He's in Miami. He came on a boat. He was one of the first boat people [*she laughs*]. He went fishing; he caught Miami. They got lost. I have an uncle that's a Korean veteran, so there was already family here. My father came to New York right away, and we came about a year later.

EDR: And when you arrived here, you went to work in a bakery?

DP: My father in Cuba had a store. He sold clothing. Here he worked in a factory. I came in August of 1961. I turned eighteen in September, so I went straight to work, and he got me a job at a company where they baked their own bread. They had their factory and offices on Twenty-third Street, and I had to wear a uniform. There was a conveyor belt, and I picked up the turnovers and other pastries and put them on a tray, then on a cart, and then delivered them.

EDR: So you were in Cuba until you were seventeen years old.

DP: Yes, I am almost sixty-one now.

EDR: Were you writing when you lived in Cuba?

DP: I started writing since I was very young. Poetry. I wrote my first poem about the town and the crabs that are very abundant there.

EDR: In Spanish?

DP: Yes. It was published in a local magazine. The beaches aren't very attractive because they're man-made beaches. Its original name is Cayo Barién. So the town was flooded often when there was a big rainfall. Anyway, I always wanted to be a writer, even though I grew up in a town that didn't have a library.

EDR: That seems quite unusual. How did that happen? Did someone in your family provide books?

DP: No. I don't know how it happened. No one in my family had books. I read a lot. My mother said I taught myself to read.

EDR: So where did the books come from?

DP: I ordered them. From Havana. I think there was a publisher named Esparza that published paperbacks for 50 cents. And school was good. I went to public school, and my teachers took [an] interest in me. I started writing poetry and short stories since I was very young.

EDR: And then when you were in the U.S., you switched to drama. How did that come about?

DP: I didn't see a play until I came to New York. My first literary adventure here was in the '60s which was, you know, la época de esa efervescencia, la época hippie, um . . . Un grupo de poetas latinos de diferentes países empezamos a. . . . (the age of that effervescence, the hippie era, um . . . A group of Latino poets from different countries started to. . . .) We did a lot of poetry readings, and we put out a little magazine, homemade, called *La Nueva Sangre* (The New Blood). The name was because we were young. At the time, Latinos, well, they were called Hispanic. We were doing something that didn't have a name then, which was performing.

EDR: Was this at the same time that some of the Nuyorican poets, like Miguel Algarín, were performing their poetry on the Lower East Side?[1]

DP: No, actually, we were before that. It was Isaac Goldenberg,[2] the Peruvian, who is known as a novelist now, and Mercedes Cortázar,[3] who is Cuban. Hicimos el primer "happening" en español ever, con un ataúd en el escenario y ahí había uno de los poetas adentro, Herminio Vargas,[4] el puertorriqueño, y cuando menos se lo esperaba la gente se levantaba la tapa y recitaba un poema. (We had the first "happening" ever in Spanish, with a coffin on the stage, and one of the poets inside it, the Puerto Rican

Herminio Vargas, and when the audience least expected it, he would lift the lid and recite a poem.)

EDR: On the street?

DP: No, en una pequeña galería de artistas Latinos. En esa época fue que se empezaron a crear los diferentes grupos artísticos latinos. (No, in a small gallery for Latino artists. Those were the days when different Latino artistic groups started to form.)

EDR: So how did you switch to drama?

DP: That was the beginning, because I loved to have the audience there and see their reaction. To me, that's the most attractive thing about the theater. I can tell if they're liking it, if they're loving it, if they're crying, or laughing when I want them to laugh. I went to a festival in Caracas. It was a huge international arts festival, and I went to cover it for a magazine. While there, I ran into a group from New York from El Teatro Duo,[5] que era el único grupo latino que estaba haciendo teatro contemporáneo, de ahora, no García Lorca y Calderón de la Barca,[6] que es lo que empezó el Repertorio Español, a hacer los clásicos. Y yo conocí al director, a los actores. Esto era en el '74, o '76. En esa época yo estaba también envuelta en el movimiento feminista, y vi mas de treinta obras, y no había ni una que era sobre el tema de la mujer, que era el tema del momento. Y conversando con Ilcatania Payan, que es la actriz dominicana, le dije cuando llegue a Nueva York, voy a escribir una obra, y escribí *Beautiful Señoritas* (which was the only Latino group doing contemporary theater, of today, not García Lorca and Calderón de la Barca, which is what the Repertorio Español was doing, the classics. And I met the director and the actors. This was in '74 or '76. During that time, I was also involved in the feminist movement, and I saw more than thirty plays, and there wasn't one dealing with women's issues, which was the issue of the day, and while talking to Ilcatania Payan, the Dominican actress, I said, "When I get to New York, I'm going to write a play." And I wrote *Beautiful Señoritas*).

EDR: This was when you were with Duo Theater?

DP: Yes, but before that I was with Teatro de Orilla, a popular theater. I didn't write anything there, but it gave me a total vision of what theater is because I had to do everything, from making the lights from tomato cans, to working at the box office. I've done everything in the theater except acting. It gives you an idea of the whole, how everything is connected.

EDR: So going back to *Beautiful Señoritas*, it's been thirty years since you wrote it. What's the audience's reaction to it now? Have stereotypes changed in a way that affects the audience's reaction to that play?

DP: Well, things have changed, but they haven't changed. I work for a magazine where we flaunt our so-called sensuality, and you know, "hotness," and you know it's empowering. So in a way that's different. But the play still works, because it's still funny. I think there's still a stereotype. And one thing about the Latino community is that there's always new people coming in, damos tres pasos 'alante y dos atrás, porque toda gente recién llegad[a] trae ciertas ideas que nos vuelven, en términos de la mujer, el rol de la mujer, vis-à-vis las relaciones. (We take three steps forward and two back, because the new immigrants bring with them certain ideas that take us back, in terms of women, the role of women, vis-à-vis relationships.)

EDR: Can you elaborate on that?

DP: The new wave of immigrants bring back some of the negatives, especially about the role of women in the marriage, que la mujer no salga a trabajar, y todo ese tipo de cosa (that a woman doesn't work outside the home, and that kind of thing). A woman's work is never done. That's a line from *Beautiful Señoritas*, and we see it at the magazine. The newcomers are now where we were thirty years ago. El machismo, drinking, et cetera.

EDR: The title of your play, *Coser y Cantar* kind of echoes the phrase you just quoted from *Beautiful Señoritas*. Where did that title come from?

DP: That was from a commercial in Cuba about the Singer sewing machine. "Con una máquina Singer, la vida es coser y cantar." ("With a Singer sewing machine, life is sewing and singing.") Meaning the life of a woman is, you know, domesticity, and sing while you sew or wash [*she laughs*], and my mother being a seamstress, tener una Singer era una gran cosa (having a Singer was a big deal). It [the play's title] comes from that. Women are happy with domesticity and not complaining. . . .

EDR: How does that saying apply to the character, "Ella," the Latina half of the woman in the play?

DP: Well, let me say that's my favorite play, because it's the most personal. I remember when my sisters went to see it when it opened. There are so many things from our lives that they told me, "Do you have to say everything about us?"

EDR: How do you see the two halves of these women at the end of the play? Are they fused together as one?

DP: Not yet. Remember that the motif of this play is looking for a man. And in a way, you're looking for guidance because you don't know how to do this. I think it's a lot easier now, for Latinas now, because we have magazines, and radio, and TV, and it's okay to be Americana but still be Latina. But when I came here, there was none of that. You sort of felt you had to become más gringa que (more gringa than [them]). My parents wanted me to learn English because they didn't want me to go through the same discrimination they went through. But now you can do both. That's freedom. You don't have to throw your culture away.

EDR: Is that what Milagros does in *Botánica*?

DP: Exactly. To bring it all together. And that's something that is individual. How you keep *She and Ella* on an even keel.

EDR: How do you see yourself or present yourself to others?

DP: I see myself as a Latina, by choice. I identify myself more as a Latina playwright than as a Cuban-American playwright because I've been rejected by my own community because of politics. It happened in Miami. My first play ever to play in Miami was a musical, *Four Guys Named José*. It was a big musical, and it was an American theme. Before that, they boycotted me for years. In 1977 and 1978, I had been to Cuba, as part of the *Diálogos, Diálogo I* and *Diálogo II*.[7] We were the first Cuban-Americans who wanted to begin a dialogue with Cubans in Cuba. I was in favor of normalizing relations with Cuba, and if Jimmy Carter had been re-elected, it probably would have happened. I mean, nothing else has worked. I wrote a piece about it called "Cuba Is a Four-letter Word," after that first trip, and I received death threats after it. Anyway, they were going to do *Coser y Cantar* in Miami, and as soon as my name was announced, one of those Miami feeding frenzies began, with bomb threats and everything. I was invited to the Excelsior Theater. They tried to disinvite me. I went anyway. It was a week of hell. Finally, the play was canceled.

EDR: Have things changed for you there?

DP: Not really. The play *Four Guys Named José* went well there. But it's not strictly a Cuban play; it's a pan-Latino play. There are four characters from different countries, and María is a pan-Latina. And it's a musical—from Ricky Ricardo to Ricky Martin. My friends tell me things have changed in Miami, but when I read the paper and hear the radio, I don't see it. And I actually believe that no matter where you're from, you are also Latina. I'm not saying that you reject your origins. If we don't join together, siempre vamos a ser los mexicanos por acá, los Cubanos por allá, et cetera (we'll always be the Mexicans over here, the Cubans over there, et cetera). We're now the majority minority, and do you see any difference? No.

EDR: How do you feel about labels in general?

DP: I'm very comfortable being a Latina, but I'd really rather be thought of as simply a playwright. When Luis Valdez's *Zoot Suit*[8] came to Broadway, the subtitle was a "New American Play." I've always said my theater is very American, because, first of all, I don't write about Cuba. I'm not there; I'm here. My plays are very American. They're about the American experience of different people, so I see myself as an American playwright.

EDR: So, do you see yourself influenced by any American playwrights or writers in general?

DP: My influences are Luis Valdez and Rogers and Hammerstein. I love musicals. I love the American musical.

EDR: Did you study writing or literature?

DP: To be a playwright, you don't need to study literature. I didn't study how to write plays. I took a workshop from Maria Irene Fornes,[9] who taught us to listen to our creative bodies. I took some literature courses at Hunter College, but that was because I was interested in literature, not to learn how to write.

EDR: Where do you get your material for your plays?

DP: From watching average people. When I teach a workshop, I focus on two things. One is character. I believe in character more than plot. If you put together two interesting people in a room, something's going to happen. And the other one is dialogue. Authentic dialogue. So, I think that you can't write a play about hunger. That's an essay. You have to write about people who are hungry. For example, with *Botánica*, I wanted to bring up the difference between the generations of immigrants, more than in *Coser y Cantar*. How you bring the two things together. So I chose the *botánica* (herbalist shop). I didn't know anything about botánicas. I didn't grow up with santería, ni collares; mi mama era muy católica (Santería [an Afro-Caribbean religion] or beads; my mother was very Catholic). But since I live in this neighborhood, most of my ideas are right here in this neighborhood. So I said, the botánica is the best example, because there are about forty botánicas en esta área (herbalist shops in this area). So, I used to go in and ask questions. They don't like you to ask questions, and I ended up buying a lot of stuff. And I thought, this is a good setting because it's extreme. To live in New York, and people still have the botánica and los despojos (the cleansings), and it's not even original from Latin America, it's from America. La abuela que es la ceiba, y Millie que está educada en la universidad de blanquitas, y que estudia banking.(The grandmother who's the ceiba tree, and Millie, who's educated in a university for "white girls," and who studies banking.) When I started writing that play, I thought I was writing Millie's play. It's one of the wonderful things about writing. Once you create characters, they take over, and you don't control them anymore. The strong character there is la abuela. El Repertorio Español[10] did that play for ten years, and when they'd bring school kids in, after the play, they all wanted to talk to the grandmother, not Millie, because everyone has a grandmother like that. I remember when they did the play in Texas. It was the first time they did a non-Mexican play, because ellos son muy de ellos nada más (because they [the Mexicans] just like doing their own thing). Y este profesor me preguntó (and this teacher asked me), "Do you think this play is going to work here?" And at the end of the play, he said, "You were right, because everyone has a grandmother like that." Never mind that la vieja es puertorriqueña, podía haber sido mexicana o otra cosa (that the old lady is Puerto Rican; she could have been Mexican or anything else).

EDR: In that play Millie asks, rhetorically, "Who are we?" Rubén answers, "We are both mangoes and strawberries." Is that who the new Latina is?

DP: Exactly. I think Rubén has it together, whereas Millie didn't.

EDR: At the end of the play, Millie uses the computer to keep records of the traditional recipes. What does that represent?

DP: The computer is like la ceiba (the ceiba tree). Se enterraban las cosas sagradas al pie de la ceiba. (You would bury sacred things at the foot of the oak.) The computer is the same.

EDR: Let's talk a bit about Cuban-American literature in general. What themes or ideas do you think make up this field?

DP: I think it's about what we lost. Everybody's loss. Being an immigrant for whatever reason means losing something. It sometimes means giving up something. We try to recreate it here, but it's not true. It's not our country. Even if you never learn English, like my mother. She watched the Spanish soap operas and lived in her own world, but it was fake. Cubans also have this thing about everyone having been rich in Cuba, and everything having been perfect.

EDR: So, you're saying that Cuban-American literature is about nostalgia? What about someone like Roberto Fernández,[11] who sees the humor in the stereotypes?

DP: He's the only one. Roberto is the one who comes closer to describing that esquizofrenia miamense (Miami-style schizophrenia). He's been doing it for a long time, but he hasn't had an impact somehow. Some of his earlier works were in Spanish and didn't translate well. It has to be done in English.

EDR: Since you bring up the issue of language, how do you decide when to use English or Spanish?

DP: Every play tells me in what language it should be written. For example, in *Pantallas* (TV Screens), que yo *quería* jugar con ese lenguaje novelesco, tenía que ser en español (where I *wanted* to play around with that "soap opera-ish" language, it had to be in Spanish).

EDR: What are you working on now?

DP: I have a lot of material that is not theater. I want to give it a try. I don't know if I have the patience to write a novel. I have a lot of pieces. Originally, I wanted to publish a book with stories, anecdotes, et cetera. So, I'm going to try to put it together as a novel.

EDR: In your work, there seems to be much criticism directed internally, at Cubans, rather than at some other external force.

DP: Being able to laugh at yourself is a sign of maturity.

EDR: How did your translations of Julia Alvarez[12] and other writers come about?

DP: Well, I know Julia Alvarez, and they had done a translation of her *How the Garcia Girls Lost Their Accent* in Spain, and it was severely criticized in the Dominican Republic. So, Julia insisted that her next book be translated by a Hispanic writer.

EDR: What do you want your audiences to come away with from your work?

DP: With a laugh, or a chuckle, at least. And a better understanding of who I am.

EDR: Back to the question posed by Millie. Who are we? Who are you?

DP: I'm a human being. A complex person made up of two languages, two cultures. When I first came here, I was appalled that people didn't know about Cuba. I mean, it was the year of the Bay of Pigs,[13] and people still asked me where Cuba was. What language we spoke in Cuba. Or they thought we danced flamenco. All of those things made me think, these people have no idea who I am. You become an image, not a human being. Everything is described as black and white. I remember when *Coser y Cantar* opened, no one thought anyone would understand the whole thing, only half, because it's in two languages. But then, a woman from Turkey told me she understood everything because she went through that.

Virgil Suárez

∴ ∴ ∴

Everything about Virgil Suárez's appearance confirms his statement in this conversation that he is a "creature of instant gratification." He arrives at my hotel in Tallahassee, Florida, in his low-rider car and informs me that this is the vehicle he loves to take to the office so he can gauge the reaction it elicits from some of his more conservative colleagues. He is wearing a pair of leather biker boots, which match his black leather vest. To say that his attire is incongruous with the atmosphere at the southern plantation-style restaurant, where we have lunch, would be a monumental understatement.

Later, as we talk in his home, it is easy to see why Suárez is one of the most prolific of all Cuban-American writers. He speaks in long bursts, on several different subjects simultaneously, and his words are usually accompanied by emphatic gestures. This energy and enthusiasm has translated into eight books of poetry, three novels, three anthologies, and a memoir. In addition, his individual works have been published in dozens of literary journals and collected in several anthologies. He has also received a National Endowment for the Arts Fellowship, in 2001, and he was awarded the Georgina MacArthur Poetry Prize in 2002.

Like the man himself, his work leaves an indelible imprint on the reader's mind. From his vivid description of the slaughtering of animals to the joyful reunion of family members at the Miami airport, his poetry is replete with images that are as memorable as the author himself is. Suárez, who was born in Havana in 1962, and left the island with his family eight years later, guides his readers through the labyrinth of memory and imagination. Because of this ability to engage the reader, Suárez's remark at the conclusion of this interview—that his literary voice will "be quiet for a while"—leads one to hope that it will be a very short silence.

The date is April 29, 2005.

Works

90 Miles (2005)

Landscapes and Dreams (2003)

Vespers: Spirituality in America (2003)

Guide to the Blue Tongue (2002)

Banyan (2001)

Palm Crows (2001)

American Diaspora (2001)

In the Republic of Longing (2000)

You Come Singing (1998)

Garabato Poems (1998)

Spared Angola (1997)

Going Under (1996)

Havana Thursdays (1995)

Iguana Dreams (1993)

Welcome to the Oasis (1992)

The Cutter (1991)

⁘

EDR: I'd like to start by talking about your poetry. You've always written poetry, since your days in L.A., so I won't ask why you've been writing poetry now instead of fiction, but rather why you've decided to return to it.

VS: I never left poetry. The earliest memory I have of writing poetry was when I was fifteen or sixteen. I had a girlfriend, and I was madly in love. I was also taking advance placement Spanish with Dr. Alvarado at Huntington Park Senior High School in Huntington, and we were reading people like Borges,[1] and I went crazy with it. I was writing poetry for the next four or five years. All of it horrible stuff. I still have some of it, and some of it I'm going to light on fire. So, I never left it. What happened was that when I went to college the first workshop that I was able to get into was a fiction writing workshop. The teacher came in, gave us an assignment, and I started writing a novel, which ended up being *The Cutter*. But all along, I was writing poetry, and I was performing poetry, so I never left it. But you know, once you start writing novels people will pigeonhole you, and that's how initially my work came out. In the mind of the reader, I was a novelist. I was a fiction writer. Very few people knew that I was writing poetry, and so, in later years, as it became more and more difficult to write fiction, I kept writing poetry and finally had it published. It was very well received. I mean, I think my first poem was published in 1987 or so. It took off, and I liked the exchange between myself and the editor. It was far better than sitting down and spending five years working on a novel that plays for three or four weeks, if you're lucky, and then it's sort of forgotten. Then it's really painful when the publisher asks if you want to buy the last few copies for ninety-three cents before they mulch them or whatever. So, I thought, "I really don't get as much pleasure as I do working on a poem, then reading it, then sending it out, then working with an editor, then revising, then putting it into a book, or getting it into an anthology or whatever." It seems to me that my poems have been around much longer than my fiction. I'm a creature of instant gratification.

EDR: Your poetic subject matter, Cuba, also hasn't changed throughout the years. Do you think your *treatment* of that subject has changed from *You Come Singing*, to the new poems you include in your book, *90 Miles*?

vs: I think it's the same in that there are people that I gravitate towards, my mother being one, and I've sort of spent the last twenty years chronicling the stories that I've heard from them. The stories about their friendships, the stories about their life in Cuba that I don't really remember living through, but I sort of live vicariously through them. I think it's a continuity of the spirit of whatever the exile community has gone through. That continuity is sort of firsthand for me in terms of family. Let me give you a couple of examples. I wrote a poem a few months ago about this lady who arrived from Cuba and never unpacked. When it became clear to her that she was going to live in exile for a long time, then she started preparing for death. She would go over the same things every day: her hair, her makeup, what she wanted for her burial, et cetera. It was a ritual that she went through for thirty years. I wrote another poem about my father, who would open tomatoes or peppers, remove the seeds, and then put them on napkins all over the house so they would dry, and then he would collect the seeds and plant them everywhere.[2] Someone brought him some seeds from Cuba and that made him really happy. So, I started thinking about the connection between vegetables and my father and living in exile, and the notion that Cuban vegetables were better than the ones from anywhere else. So, the spirit of what I write is always the same, and it's really not going to change because this is the material. This is what I care to write about.

EDR: Let's talk about language. Your work is written primarily in English. Even some of your poems with Spanish titles, like "El Exilio" from *Palm Crows* or "Gallos Finos" from *In the Republic of Longing*, are written in English. Do you feel English is a necessary tool of Cuban-American literature as it relates to the sense of exile and loss?

vs: I got very used to writing in English because Spanish has never been a very comfortable language for me. It's not a language that I feel I've mastered or know. I like playing games, so the fact that in English you can write the same image five different times in different ways appeals to me. I also think that English has served as a filter between my memories of Cuba and my life here. It's sort of a bridge, but it's a long bridge that I have to take every day. I don't like the way Spanish feels in my mind when I'm writing. I think that has to do with a lot of poems I read [early in my life] by Neruda,[3] which to me now sound extremely sappy and romantic. I've always been able to keep Spanish at bay and not let it get too much into the work, because it just doesn't sound right. I get very

self-conscious about my Spanish when I write. It's the language of my
parents, and English has always provided me a nice safe place where I
didn't feel someone was looking over my shoulder or being judgmental.
I remember leaving my journals around and never worrying that my
parents were going to pick them up and say "Whoa, what's this?" or
something like that. So, it gives me a little bit of a distance, and it allows
me to lie.

EDR: Are there any other factors in addition to language that you
feel define Cuban-American literature?

VS: I like a clear focus on the island, on diaspora. There should be
enough clues so you can say that it's about Cuban matters. We haven't
gotten to the point where Cuban-American writers feel comfortable
enough writing mystery novels, though there are a couple. Carolina
Aguilera,[4] I think her name is, she's Cuban, and she's writing a mystery
novel. Is that going to be part of Cuban-American literature? I don't
think so. So, it's not just language, but also subject matter. I think it's
about the convergence of the old world and the new world, as people
play it in the United States, whether it's in exile, or whether it's in joining
the mainstream. These are the handles that I would put on the definition of Cuban-American literature so that it's manageable. If not, it
has to include the first years of the dissidents coming and writing their
memoirs.

EDR: What about the idea that Pérez Firmat[5] proposes regarding the
hyphen? That Cuban-Americans live life in the middle of two cultures.
This seems to suggest a tension between cultures, as well as describing Cuban-Americans as a homogeneous "group," with no distinctions
between them. Can you speak to that?

VS: Well, that applies to him and people like him, as "one-and-a-
halfers."[6] My generation is the next one, and then, the next one, which
includes my children. For me, the work has to deal with the subject
matter of Cuba in some way. That's what I always come back to.

EDR: In fact, much of your work relies on your re-creation of the
Cuba you remember. How does memory work as a theme in your work?
How are memory and nostalgia related?

VS: I remember when I started writing. I started writing from memory. It's what facilitates the work. I'll remember an image, and then I'll
go back in there and start to craft something that will resemble a poem,
or an essay, or whatever. So, it's important to me to be able to remember

something specific. The trick is tapping into the communal nostalgia of what the thing itself represents. I always tell stories in my poems and link a lot of images in my poems, because it's an organic way I've found to avoid feeling that this is just another poem about nostalgia. I don't want the nostalgia to lead to sentimentality. I don't want someone to read it and get sad, or whatever. I use nostalgia to tap into whatever texture remains about the things that I think about. It's a tool, not an end. Without memory, I don't think I would have anything to say. To me, it's about an individual memory, not a communal one. I would say that whatever happened to the community sinks into my work whenever I find a parallel to it in my own life.

EDR: Let's talk a bit about your own life then. You left Cuba in 1970, but arrived in the U.S., specifically California, about four years later. Can you talk about that experience?

VS: We went from Havana to Madrid and then we arrived in Los Angeles in 1974. I was about thirteen. The school's administration brought me down a grade. I didn't speak any English, so they put me in with a lot of Mexican kids. I immediately got a taste of the kind of blanketing that takes place in most Anglo communities, where, by the nature of the proximity of Mexican kids, everyone assumed I was Mexican. There's also the whole issue of being labeled a wetback. The interesting thing was that I and the Mexican kids would play soccer with basketballs because there was no soccer in schools then. It was sort of my introduction into the mainstream culture—that there are things you bring into the mainstream culture that are not appreciated or respected. That sort of set up this model for later in my life.

EDR: What are your early memories of Cuba?

VS: My father bought a house about 20 kilometers from the center of Havana. My father had been a policeman, so when the revolution came, he hid behind the new profession that he undertook of a pattern cutter. I mean, not because he had done anything wrong, but simply because he had worked for the government. As the revolution took hold, we started taking in animals in [the backyard of] our house, chickens and pigs. It was a really weird way of having nature come into the city.

EDR: Much of your work deals with animals, the slaughtering of animals, in particular. Is that where those images come from?

VS: Yes, my father had been raised in the country but was sent to Havana to live with one of his uncles at a fairly early age. When things got real bad after the revolution, he started going out "foraging," which was the word he always used to explain how he would come home with boxes of writhing things. One time he came home with these turtles. So, here's this man who really has no idea what to do with these turtles, but he figures, there's thirty turtles, or however many, and it's meat. Maybe he remembered eating turtle when he was a farm boy. I helped him slaughter the turtles. With a ladle, I'd pull on their beaks and he'd chop off the head with a machete. It was brutal, of course, but I don't really blame my father for it. I mean, how else do you eat the turtle meat? It was a different kind of killing than the killing that I saw later when I would go over to my grandfather's farm. That was more methodical and also magical at the same time. My grandmother would get a box of rice, lure the chicken by offering it some rice, and then wring its neck. So there was a connection between the killing and food on the table. With my father, it was different, in that I wasn't used to eating rabbit, or goat, or turtle meat. As things became more stringent in Cuba, we started doing that. He would sometimes trade the animals in for other things, like coffee. But other times, we'd kill the animals. These were things that I never forget, but it made sense because my father always explained that we needed these animals to eat.

EDR: In *Spared Angola*, you often make the connection between the death of an animal, or a tree, like in "La Ceiba," and the death of Cuba.

VS: Correct. It is the death of your culture. Whether Cuba in the '50s was a golden age or not, I don't know. But Cubans of that time had a sense that they were involved in high culture. Cuba always had great literature, great film, great theater. After the revolution that clock starts winding itself back, so what you have, for the most part, is very learned people thrown into conditions of squalor. This is how you take a policeman and his new bride and his son in a very nice suburb, and within ten years, you see it erode to where he's keeping animals in the backyard. So, you see this world diminish and become more rural, more violent, and there are people relying on whatever they have at their disposal to make a go of it. Every book that I have seen of Havana in the last twenty years shows a crumbling city. That's the irony of the revolution that tells you, "We're going to bring you into the future," and really, what's happened is they've been taken back into the past.

EDR: How are *Spared Angola*'s tone and structure related? It seems to me that while the structure is linear, boyhood to adulthood, the tone is circular: from fondness to angst, and then, ultimately, back to fondness (maybe acceptance is better). Is this accurate?

vs: I think what you suggest fits as an overall description, but I also think that most of what I think when I write, especially *Spared Angola*, is a collage. I really don't think that there is a linear frame that you can apply to my work. It's not that I'm trying to capture the essentials of what it means to be an exile. I like to feel that on a daily basis, at my disposal, I have a whole world of possibilities. So, never mind going from work to work, my mood changes from one hour to the next, and I like to be able to either sit down and write my poem, or sit down and think, "Well, it's no longer a poem, it's an essay." And I think that's how *Spared Angola* came about, and why I feel comfortable enough including the poetry, because the poems include these little gaps, these little snippets, that wouldn't have fit otherwise. In my mind, though, they were part of the whole picture. The book is basically a mosaic of different moments in my life.

EDR: In addition to *Spared Angola*, some of the imagery in your other works is equally memorable. For instance, in your book of poems, *90 Miles*, you call Cuba "the island of suspended disbelief." What did you mean by that?

vs: That comes from the experience I had reading *A View of Dawn in the Tropics* by Cabrera Infante,[7] which is a book that I read early in my life. I remember reading that book and just loving the fact that in it, he combines everything: history, politics, myth, fable. And it's also that he calls it a fiction, but it really isn't a fiction. It collapses time, so that you get Cuban history in a linear way, but it's also scattered along. And you also sort of have to make certain leaps of faith to get there, to get at the beauty of that book. It's in the scope of Faulkner. Or even what Juan Rulfo does in *Pedro Páramo*.[8] And probably a little bit of Benítez Rojo's *Repeating Island*.[9] We will reenter Cuba and start living the life of our parents or our grandparents. And in that way, we're sort of ghosts in our own lives. Because we've been yearning for this moment, and, I think, luckily in our generation, it'll arrive. You will be able to visit with your parents. You will be able to visit with your grandparents. I was also thinking of this one time [when] I went to someone's house, and he had Marilyn Monroe footage that they were projecting at the bottom of the swimming pool. I thought, "That's what it's going to be like going back to Cuba." It's the reality of going back, but it'll be layered with all of these moments. All of these memories. And I think you'll have to be ready to not only suspend disbelief, but to leap forward and backwards. It'll be time coming to a standstill, and reliving everything again.

EDR: In addition to Cabrera Infante, what other writers had an influence on you?

VS: Well, Lezama Lima, Virgilio Piñero, Severo Sarduy.[10] People like that. From the early stuff, it would have to be Cirilo Villaverde.[11] Of the new people coming out of Cuba, I just don't know. I haven't been reading the new Cuban literature. I've looked at the poetry of Nancy Morejón,[12] but I haven't been keeping up with what's going on right now in Cuban letters. It's hard to keep up with that because there's so much stuff going on here.

EDR: Let's switch a moment and talk about labels. How do you identify yourself? Latino, Cuban, Cuban-American, Cuban Exile? Are these distinctions important in literary studies?

VS: I remember Roberto Fernández telling me, "Be careful with the mainstream, because the mainstream can reward you initially, but then they'll drop you and forget about you. You want to work towards becoming a classic." He meant by that that when you get scholars to get interested in you, then you enter a different arena, and that will last. Who were the Pulitzer-prize winning novelists of the 1920s? Most of them are gone. Most of them have disappeared. I think [that] at the end of the day, I don't mind being called a Cuban-American, because I think it's sort of a way to become immortal, in that eventually, whether somebody thinks I'm great or I'm terrible, they will at least put me in a footnote somewhere. And I really like that.

EDR: In addition to being an author, you are an important editor of Latino literature and of Cuban-American literature, in particular. What guidelines do you use when selecting Cuban authors for your anthologies?

VS: The process is a template. I strive for balance between the established and the very new. I like to include new people, but I also want to showcase the masters. I also want gender equity. There are plenty of women writers, and I want to make sure people know this. I also want to make sure I have a balance of genres. Finally, I try to keep the reader in mind. What do they want to read?

EDR: Your anthology *Iguana Dreams* was published in 1993. How has Cuban-American literature changed in the last thirteen years? Do you see it as part of the American literary canon? Will it ever be in the mainstream?

vs: I think Cuban-American literature is beginning to enter the mainstream, and some individual writers, like Cristina García,[13] have already done so. So, I think it's developed quite a bit. But my fear is that we're in a bit of a standstill. There are *some* new writers, but we're a bit stagnant. In the next few years, there may be a new wave. I'm sure they're coming.

EDR: I'd like to end our conversation by asking about your current work. Anything being published soon?

vs: My latest work is a sequence of new poems about Elián González. It's done, but I won't publish it for a while. I'm still waiting to hear more about the reception of my last book. Right now, I'm working on a collection of short stories not previously published called *The Soviet Circus Comes to Havana*. After that I plan to be quiet for a while.

.·. .·. .·.

Epilogue

As I reread the interviews collected here, and remember the meetings with these authors, what strikes me most is how unique each of them truly is. At first, this seems like a trivial, inconsequential observation. However, when I consider that a crucial part of my mission was to collect a group of "similar" writers all of whom left Cuba as children or young adults, their divergence forces me to examine this issue more closely.

Virgil Suárez and Roberto Fernández are professors at the same institution, Florida State University in Tallahassee, albeit in different departments (English and Modern Languages, respectively). "Surely they must be pals and get together frequently for barbeques," I imagined as I traveled to that city. Although they are friends, it is truly difficult to picture them together in an informal setting. Suárez would probably be motioning wildly with a drumstick in his hand, while Fernández quietly watches from a distance with an amused look on his face. Their work, like their personalities, could not be more dissimilar. Suárez employs striking images in a serious attempt to explore the conflict in the Cuban-American identity, while Fernández uses humor to illustrate the absurdity of that conflict.

The verse of poets Dionisio Martínez and Ricardo Pau-Llosa are similar in nature, both being highly intellectual and philosophical. They have no interest in drawing from, or evoking, simple emotion. They both create series of metaphors that not only build one on another, but often, paradoxically, produce a number of unrelated ideas. "Surely," I think, "these two writers must have somewhat similar personalities." Nothing could be further from the truth. Pau-Llosa's clothes, demeanor, and home reveal his penchant for the finer things in life, while Martínez conveys a more austere character.

The four women I interviewed all create female characters, in poetry or prose, that defy Latina stereotypes. Yet, each of them has her own unique style in both her writing and demeanor. Dolores Prida and Achy Obejas both oppose the U.S. embargo on Cuba, but there the similarities end. Prida speaks in a calm, almost wistful style, while Obejas is full of uncontrollable energy. Carolina Hospital and Cristina García left Cuba at almost the same age, yet they have had very different life experiences. García is a professional journalist who has transformed herself into a successful novelist, while Hospital is an educator, scholar, and poet.

Both Nilo Cruz and Eduardo Machado are successful playwrights living and working in New York City. There the similarities end. Cruz's work focuses on the lives of everyday people. The plays of Eduardo Machado sketch what life is like in mostly white, educated, upper-class Cuban society. Both men are a reflection of their work, as Cruz, in dress and mannerism, is relaxed and laid back, while Machado is much more formal in speech and appearance.

About all that Pablo Medina and Gustavo Pérez Firmat have in common is that they both teach in New York. Even then, Pérez Firmat spends only part of his time in that city because he flies home every week to North Carolina. In poetry and prose, Medina chronicles the lives of crises-riddled Cuban-Americans, while Pérez Firmat, although a fiction writer, is best known as a literary critic.

It seems appropriate, therefore, that this book be titled *One Island, Many Voices*. Although I may have helped delineate what does and does not constitute Cuban-American literature, as I recall the interviews with these twelve writers, I am reminded that any such analysis is inclusive and limiting. The fact that these writers can be grouped together because they share a hyphenated existence only partially illuminates the wide-ranging kaleidoscope of styles, genres, and themes that truly defines Cuban-American literature.

:•: :•: :•:

Notes

Introduction

1. Hospital, *Cuban American Writers*.

2. Smorkaloff, *Cuban Writers on and off the Island*.

3. Bruce-Novoa, *Chicano Authors*.

4. Hernández, *Puerto Rican Voices*.

5. Alvarez-Borland, *Cuban-American Literature*.

6. Pérez Firmat, *Life on the Hyphen*, p. 5. He takes the more widely used term "American-bred Cuban" and reverses it, in an attempt to emphasize that the only part of these people that is truly Cuban is that they were born to Cuban parents.

7. Alvarez-Borland, *Cuban-American Literature*, pp. 7, 8.

8. Among the other critics who have grappled with this definition are Eliana Rivero ("From Immigrants to Ethnics") and Juan Bruce-Novoa.

9. Born in New York City to Cuban parents, Hijuelos is perhaps best known for his Pulitzer Prize–winning novel, *The Mambo Kings Play Songs of Love*. Menéndez has published a collection of short stories, *In Cuba I Was a German Shepherd* and more recently a novel, *Loving Che*. Richard Blanco's first book, *City of a Hundred Fires*, won the University of Pittsburgh Agnes Starrett Prize, and his second book, *Directions to the Beach of the Dead*, was published by the University of Arizona Press in 2005.

10. Pérez Firmat, *Life on the Hyphen*, p. 137.

11. The only exception here may be Dolores Prida, who arrived in the United States at age eighteen.

12. The title of a recent collection of essays on Spanish American and Latino literature edited by Jorge Febles, *Into the Mainstream: Essays on Spanish American and Latino Literature and Culture* underscores this point.

13. Three examples produced within the last seven years are del Rio, *The Prentice Hall Anthology of Latino Literature*; Kanellos, *Herencia: The Anthology of Hispanic Literature of the United States*; and Christie and Gonzalez, eds., *Latino Boom: An Anthology of U.S. Latino Literature*.

14. Pérez Firmat, *Life on the Hyphen*, p. 8.

15. For Rivero, Puerto Rican and Chicano literature are both more concerned with the working class than is Cuban-American literature, and she thus views the former writings as opposed to, rather than assimilated into, the dominant culture.

16. In the Aztec people's native tongue, Nahuatl, the word *Aztlán* refers to the mythical place of origin. The term *xicanindio*, a combination of Mexican and Indian,

emerged as part of a project by the same name, which is now Arizona's oldest Native and Hispanic arts organization. Some people use the term to refer to their combined Chicano and Native heritage.

17. Rivero, "Hispanic Literature in the United States," p. 184.

18. Caminero-Santangelo, "Contesting the Boundaries of 'Exile' Latino/a Literature," p. 507.

19. They are Pérez Firmat, Obejas, Medina, Fernández, Suárez, and García.

20. See, for example, Mary S. Vasquez, "Cuba as Text and Context in Cristina Garcia's *Dreaming in Cuban*," *Bilingual Review* 20, no. 1: 22–28; Katherine B. Payant, "From Alienation to Reconciliation in the Novels of Cristina Garcia," *MELUS* 26, no. 3 (2001): 163–82; and Maya Socolovsky, "Unnatural Violences: Counter-Memory and Preservations in Cristina Garcia's *Dreaming in Cuban* and *The Agüero Sisters*," *Literature, Interpretation, Theory* 11, no. 2 (2000): 143–67.

21. Luis, *Dance Between Two Cultures*, p. 148. In this seminal study, Luis examines not only the literature of Cuban-Americans like Ricardo Pau-Llosa and Gustavo Pérez Firmat, but he places that literature within its social, political, and historical context.

22. The 1970s marked a lessening of tensions between the United States and Cuba. In 1974 and 1975, several U.S. senators traveled to Cuba, and upon returning, they called for the lifting of the embargo. These attempts at normalization, at least officially, were halted when Cuba sent troops to Angola in 1976. See the interview with Prida.

Nilo Cruz

1. At the center of the play is the *lector*, or reader, who would read newspapers and novels to the cigar rollers as they worked. This nineteenth-century tradition was exported from Cuba to the factories in Tampa and Ybor City, Florida.

2. Cuba's national treasure, Martí was a tireless advocate of Cuba's independence from Spain. He was imprisoned for his revolutionary ideas and subsequently exiled. From 1881 to 1895, he lived in New York, where he continued to write, and where he also established the Cuban Revolutionary Party and the daily journal, *Patria*.

3. Although primarily known as a playwright, Piñera published essays, short stories, novels, and poetry. He was born in the Cuban province of Matanzas, the birthplace of Cruz, in 1912. His plays have been performed in several Latin American and European countries, and he was awarded the prestigious Premio Casa de las Américas in 1968. He died in Havana in 1979.

4. Novelist Reinaldo Arenas committed suicide in 1990 after being diagnosed with AIDS three years earlier. His haunting tale of persecution and imprisonment in Cuba because of his gay lifestyle was published in English in 1993 as *Before Night Falls*.

5. Considered an enemy of the right-wing forces during the Civil War, Spanish poet and playwright Federico García Lorca was executed in 1936 without ever going to trial. *The House of Bernarda Alba*, published posthumously in 1945, depicts a love triangle involving the two daughters of the title character.

6. Literally "worm." Used by Castro supporters as a pejorative label to identify Cubans who rejected the regime.

7. Cuban-born Maria Irene Fornes is an internationally acclaimed director, playwright, and teacher. All three playwrights interviewed in this collection attribute their success to Fornes's instruction and guidance.

8. *Beauty of the Father* was first produced in early 2004 at the New Theater in Coral Gables, Florida. In the conversation, Cruz means here that he is continuing to work on the script, before its New York debut, which would take place in January 2006, at the Manhattan Theater Club, off Broadway.

Roberto Fernández

1. Meaning "the daring ones," an appellation taken from a groundbreaking anthology edited by Carolina Hospital, *Cuban American Writers: Los Atrevidos*. Hospital argued that the group of Cuban-American writers in her book had dared to go against expectations by writing and publishing in English. See the interview with Hospital.

2. One of the giants of Cuban literature, Guillermo Cabrera Infante was a one-time supporter of Castro's government. While a cultural attaché in Belgium, his sentiments turned against the regime, however. His writing style, reminiscent of James Joyce, is perhaps best illustrated in his 1967 novel *Tres Tristes Tigres*.

3. Fernandez is referring to information peculiar to a particular culture that allows those familiar with it (that is, those who have the database) to understand its nuances.

4. See the Introduction, note 9.

5. Both Fernández and Suárez are included in the 2006 *Southern Writers: A New Biographical Dictionary*. See the interview with Virgil Suárez.

Cristina García

1. García, ed., *Bordering Fires*. The writing of the Mexican authors was translated into English for publication in *Bordering Fires*, and simultaneously, the Chicano authors' works were translated into Spanish for publication in Mexico, in the volume titled, *Voces sin fronteras*.

2. The Ten Years War started in 1868, when Carlos Manuel de Céspedes, a Cuban landowner, freed his slaves in protest of Spain's refusal to meet demands for independence. It ended after promises were made by the Spanish government, promises that were never kept. The Cuban War of Independence officially lasted three years (1895–1888), but the Cuban Republic was not founded until May 20, 1902, when the United States, which had helped liberate the country and had secured its rights from Spain, turned over its leadership to Cuban-elected officials. The war itself was led by José Martí (see the Cruz interview, note 2), who, unfortunately, was killed in one of its initial battles.

3. The legend of the monkey king, which dates back to about 600 AD, tells of a supernatural hero born out of stone. The tale was first recorded by a Chinese scholar in the sixteenth century.

4. The Chinese Cultural Revolution lasted roughly ten years, between 1969 and the late 1970s. It began as a rebellion against Communist Party officials by Chinese students and workers.

5. See López, ". . . And There Is Only My Imagination Where Our History Should Be: An Interview with Cristina Garcia," p. 102.

6. It is interesting to note that at least three of the authors included in this collection cite Stevens's work as a source of influence.

7. See the Introduction, note 9.

8. She is discussing *A Handbook to Luck*, published in 2007.

Carolina Hospital

1. Adopting the name Nuyorican as a reference to both the city and their Puerto Rican origins, these poets were part of the Beat Generation, and they include such figures as Miguel Algarín and Pedro Pietri.

2. See the García interview, note 2.

3. Ilan Stavans has published several books on Latin American and Latino culture. In *Spanglish: The Making of a New American Language*, he traces the development of this hybrid language.

4. This poem first appeared in *Los Atrevidos*, and it has been published subsequently in several anthologies of Latino literature.

5. Hospital is probably referring to García's *Monkey Hunting*, a large portion of which is set in the Cuban capital. See the interview with García.

6. At the time of Hospital's interview, Medina had just published *The Return of Felix Nogara*. His most recent effort is *The Cigar Roller*. See the Medina interview for a discussion of his work.

7. Castillo, *My Father Sings, To My Embarrassment*.

8. Poet Heberto Padilla was a long-time supporter of the Castro government. When the regime accused him of subversive activities and imprisoned him in 1971, an outcry came from the literary and cultural elite, including such figures as Jean-Paul Sartre and Octavio Paz. That led to Padilla's release and exile, in 1980, to the United States, where he died in 2000. For Reinaldo Arenas, see the Cruz Interview, note 4. Poet Roberto Valero is noted for his verse denouncing Fidel Castro's regime. After leaving Cuba in 1980, he received a PhD from Georgetown University, and he has published several collections of Spanish poetry, as well as a novel, *Este viento de cuaresma*, released shortly before his death in 1994.

Eduardo Machado

1. Between 1960 and 1962, amid rumors that the regime would indoctrinate Cuba's youth or even send them to Soviet work camps, parents made the difficult decision to send their unaccompanied children to Miami. Approximately 14,000 made the trip, with many ending up in orphanages or foster homes throughout the United States.

2. One of Havana's municipalities, located in the eastern part of the city.

3. See the Cruz interview, note 7.

4. In 1991, four of Machado's plays, *The Modern Ladies of Guanabacoa, Fabiola, Broken Eggs*, and *In the Eye of the Hurricane*, were collected and published as *The Floating Island Plays*.

5. This dessert consists of delicate poached meringues floating on a pool of custard sauce, with a web of caramel drizzled over it. Machado's penchant for the culinary arts has led him to publish a memoir that includes Cuban recipes, *Tastes Like Cuba: An Exile's Hunger for Home*.

6. Literally, palate. During the past several years, the Cuban government has allowed a smattering of privately owned, small restaurants, called *paladares*, to operate. They are usually in private homes that have been converted into eateries.

Dionisio Martínez

1. See Hospital interview, note 8.

2. Ira Sadoff is the Dana Professor of Poetry at Colby College in Waterville, Maine. He has published over three hundred individual poems in various literary journals, as well as six poetry collections.

3. A sequence of six, six-line stanzas in which the end words of the first stanza recur as end words of the following five stanzas.

4. A fixed form consisting of varying four-line stanzas with lines rhyming alternately. The second and fourth lines are repeated to form the first and third line of the next stanza, but in reverse order. Thus, the first and last lines of the poem are identical.

5. Pulitzer Prize–winning poet Jorie Graham was born in New York City in 1950. Her latest effort, *Never*, was published by HarperCollins in 2002. She is currently the Boylston Professor of Rhetoric and Oratory at Harvard.

6. The interview by Alison Young, *In the Front Row*, aired on November 14, 2005, on KUHF in Houston, Texas.

7. Two of these critics are Bill Christophersen ("Down from the Tower: Poetry as Confabulation") and Patrick Mackie ("The Low Style").

Pablo Medina

1. The questions and answers dealing with Medina's *The Cigar Roller* (2005) took place via e-mail in the spring of 2006.

2. Parra's first book of verse, *Cancionero sin nombre* (1937), established this Chilean poet as a major force in contemporary Latin American letters.

3. Yglesia's books on the subject include *A Wake in Ybor City* and *Guns in the Closet* (reissued posthumously in 1996). Ferdie Pacheco's most notable work on life in this Florida town is *Ybor City Chronicles*.

4. The title of this work is *Points of Balance/Puntos de apoyo*.

5. Nuyorican, a term that combines the names of the city of New York and the Commonwealth of Puerto Rico. The term was first coined by Lower East Side poets in the 1960s, such as Miguel Algarín and Pedro Pietri.

6. Medina is referring to Orestes Lorenzo, the Cuban Air Force major, who in 1992 borrowed a Cessna and returned to Cuba to rescue his family. Amazingly, he had defected a mere twenty-one months earlier in a stolen Soviet-built MiG.

7. Carpentier is widely acknowledged as the father of magical realism. His works influenced several generations of writers. He died in exile in France in 1980.

8. Colombian Nobel laureate García Márquez is perhaps best known for his novel *One Hundred Years of Solitude*, published in 1970.

9. Portuguese writer born in 1922 in Lisbon who won the Nobel Prize for Literature in 1998.

10. For more on the historical Cuban presence in New York, see the Introduction to this volume. Novelist Villaverde, born in 1812, escaped imprisonment in Havana and went into exile in the United States. He died in New York City in 1894. For

more on Martí, see the Cruz interview, note 2. Varela, ordained as a Catholic priest in Cuba, lobbied for the abolition of slavery in the 1820s. As a result, he was forced to seek refuge in New York, where he established several schools and published books and newspapers.

11. See the Fernández interview, note 2.

12. See the interview with Gustavo Pérez Firmat.

13. Vladimir Nabokov, Russian-born American novelist, perhaps best known for his novel *Lolita*, published in 1955.

14. See Hospital interview, note 8.

Achy Obejas

1. See the interview with Cristina García.

2. Mexican-American writer Sandra Cisneros is one of the dominant voices in Latino literature today. Her groundbreaking novel *The House on Mango Street* is one of the most popular books in the United States written by a Latina writer. This poem is from her collection, *My Wicked, Wicked Ways*, p. 23.

3. Puerto Rican playwright and poet Tato Laviera was born in Santurce, Puerto Rico, in 1951, and he migrated to New York with his family when he was nine years old. His book *La Carreta Made a U-Turn* is considered by many critics to be his most influential work.

4. U.S. policy, instituted in 1966, establishing that all Cubans who reach American soil are allowed to remain. In 1995, the Clinton administration reinterpreted the policy in a much narrower way. Now known as the "wet feet, dry feet" policy, Cubans who have not *literally* set foot on U.S. soil are returned to the island.

5. See the Pérez Firmat interview.

6. A Hebrew term referring to Jews who were forced to convert to Christianity during the Spanish Inquisition.

7. The ten days between Rosh Hashanah and Yom Kippur, during which the Almighty is deciding who will be written up in the Book of Life.

8. In 1980, Fidel Castro allowed Cubans to flee the island, departing from Mariel Harbor, which gave the exodus its name. As many as 125,000 people may have left. It is believed that this was a ploy by Castro to rid the island of unwanted citizens, such as criminals and mental patients.

Ricardo Pau-Llosa

1. Pau-Llosa's interest in this modern American poet (1879–1955) is due to Stevens's focus on the local while integrating the imaginative experience.

2. West Indian playwright and poet who was awarded the Nobel Prize in 1992.

3. American poet Richard Wilbur was born in New York City in 1921. His poetic style is reminiscent of Wallace Stevens. All three—Stevens, Walcott, and Wilbur—emphasize the imaginative element in their work.

4. Austro-German poet Rainer Maria Rilke was born in Prague in 1875. His *Duino Elegies* and *Sonnets to Orpheus* (both poetic cycles completed in 1923) are his greatest achievements.

5. This quote is from an interview with Pau-Llosa, conducted by Alberto Milián in 2001.

6. Both Sexton and Plath are known for their highly personal poetry and their tragic lives that ended in suicide.

7. Cuban-born historian Carlos Eire won the 2003 National Book Award for Non-Fiction for *Waiting for Snow in Havana.*

8. Early twentieth-century German philosopher Edmund Husserl is considered the father of phenomenology, a system that emphasizes the real and the observable, or, to use the vernacular, what is "encountered."

9. This remark appeared in Kandell, "Miami: City of Exiles" in *Cigar Aficionado.*

10. Betty Friedan (1921–2006) championed women's rights for over forty years. She was the co-founder of the National Organization for Women and published many articles and books, including an autobiography *Life So Far.*

11. A long instrumental solo, usually associated with percussion.

12. Cuban singer Lupe Raymond, known as "La Lupe," was a major Latin musical force in the 1960s and '70s. She was so popular that a performance at Carnegie Hall in 1969 sold out. Elena Burque was a cabaret singer in the 1950s and '60s, known for her beautiful ballads. The King of Rhythm, Benny Moré, is a Cuban musical legend who epitomized the big-band Afro-Cuban sound of the 1950s.

Gustavo Pérez Firmat

1. Literally, about "father, country, and prostate" or to attempt to retain his alliteration, "patriarchy, patriotism, and prostate." Unfortunately, much of Pérez Firmat's clever use of puns and alliteration is lost in translation.

2. Innards, obviously in a metaphorical sense.

3. See the Fernández interview.

4. See the Medina interview, note 13.

5. In his book, *Life on the Hyphen*, Pérez Firmat uses this term to describe the generation of Cuban immigrants, especially writers, who came to the United States at a very young age. They are, thus, on the hyphen between the generations.

6. Part of the Mariel exodus of 1980, Rosales committed suicide in Miami three years later. His book, *Boarding Home* (1987) was reissued by a Spanish publisher in 2003 under the title *La casa de los náufragos.*

7. Peruvian critic José Miguel Oviedo has published more than fifteen books on Latin American literature. His *Historia de la literatura hispanoamericana,* to which Pérez Firmat refers, was published in 2000.

8. In the Introduction to this book, I discuss my reasons for the omission of certain writers, such as Hijuelos (see also note 9 in that Introduction).

9. Philosopher and essayist George Santayana was born in Madrid in 1863. Despite never renouncing his Spanish citizenship, Santayana was extremely proud of his self-identification as an American writer, as Pérez Firmat observes.

10. Novelist Joseph Conrad (1857–1924) recounted his travels in works such as *Heart of Darkness* and *Lord Jim.*

11. Cuban literary critic Jorge Mañach was born in Sagua La Grande in 1898 and died in exile in Puerto Rico in 1961. His studies of José Martí (such as *Martí, el Apóstol*) are renowned for their insight.

12. Argentinean writer Jorge Luis Borges is considered one of the greatest literary figures of the twentieth century, and his work is often cited as a premier source for

the magical realism that infuses much of contemporary Latino literature.

13. José Lezama Lima was born in Havana in December, 1910. Although his novel *Paradiso* (1966) brought him international acclaim, he had spent much of his early career writing poetry. The unfinished continuation of *Paradiso*, titled *Oppiano Licario*, was published posthumously in 1977.

14. See Fernández interview, note 2.

15. Poet Alejandra Pizarnik was born in Buenos Aires, Argentina, in 1936. In the 1960s, she lived in Paris, where she published much of her poetry, as well as critical essays on various renowned literary figures. She died from an overdose in 1972.

16. See the Introduction, note 9.

17. Poet Richard Blanco was born in Madrid shortly after his mother arrived there from Cuba. See also the Introduction, note 9.

18. See the interviews with Roberto Fernández, Virgil Suárez, and Ricardo Pau-Llosa.

19. Christmas Eve.

20. Cisneros, "Dulzura," in *Loose Woman*, p. 27.

21. See the Author Headnote for Pérez Firmat in del Rio, *The Prentice Hall Anthology of Latino Literature* (New York: Prentice Hall, 2002).

22. *Picadillo* is a dish made of ground beef and chopped onions.

Dolores Prida

1. See the Hospital interview, note 1, and the Medina interview, note 5.

2. Goldenberg is a poet and novelist living in New York City. His books include *La vida contado, Tiempo al tiempo*, and *La vida a plazos de Jacobo Lerner*.

3. Mercedes Cortázar is a poet, novelist, translator, and literary critic. She is perhaps best known for her work on the Gregory Rabassa translation of Lezama Lima's *Paradiso*.

4. An educator, playwright, essayist and poet, Vargas has published several books of poems, and some of his plays have been staged in the United States and abroad.

5. Now known as the Duo Multicultural Arts Center located on East Fourth Street in New York City.

6. Spanish poet and dramatist Federico García Lorca (1898–1936) and Spanish Golden Age playwright Pedro Calderón de la Barca (1600–1681).

7. See the Introduction, note 22.

8. Valdez is considered by most critics as the father of Mexican-American theater. His creation of the theater group Teatro Campesino will ensure his place as one of the most powerful voices of the Mexican-American literary tradition.

9. See the Cruz interview, note 7.

10. Repertorio Español was founded in 1968. It aims to introduce the best of Latin American, Spanish, and Hispanic-American theater to a broad audience.

11. See the interview with Roberto Fernández.

12. Renowned New York-born Dominican novelist. Alvarez's works also include *In The Name of Salome* and her recently published *Saving the World*.

13. In 1961, approximately 1,300 Cuban exiles, backed by the CIA, stormed the beaches of Cuba. The attack was a total failure, and it resulted in the deaths of 114 of the counterrevolutionaries and the imprisonment of the rest.

Virgil Suárez

1. See the Pérez Firmat interview, note 12.

2. Suárez is referring, respectively, to "Cousin Irene" (from *The Republic of Longing*) and "The Seed Collector" (from *90 Miles*).

3. Poet Pablo Neruda was born in Chile in 1904. He was a prolific writer who was also involved in national and international politics. He was awarded the Nobel Prize in Literature in 1971, two years before his death.

4. Novelist Carolina García-Aguilera has published a series of popular novels centered around a female private investigator.

5. See the interview with Gustavo Pérez Firmat.

6. The reference here is to Pérez Firmat's *Life on the Hyphen*. His definition would still apply to Suárez, as he was born in Cuba but raised in the United States. Suárez makes a distinction that may be based more on the time at which each left the island, since Pérez Firmat's family fled in 1960, whereas Suárez's family did not go until 1970. The two are also separated in age by approximately fourteen years.

7. See the Fernández interview, note 2.

8. Novelist and short-story writer Juan Rulfo was born in the Mexican state of Jalisco in 1917. *Pedro Páramo* describes the interaction between its central character, Juan Preciado, and the ghosts of a small town.

9. Cuban writer Antonio Benítez Rojo was born in Havana in 1931 and died in exile in Massachusetts in 2005. The book to which Suárez refers is *La isla que se repite*, which won the 1993 Modern Language Association Kovacs Prize and was translated into English in 1996.

10. For Lezama Lima, see the Pérez Firmat interview, note 13. Piñera, born in the Cuban province of Matanzas in 1912, published essays, short stories, novels, and poetry, although he was primarily known as a playwright, and his plays have been performed in several Latin American and European countries. He received the prestigious Premio Casa de las Américas in 1968. He died in Havana in 1979. Sarduy died of AIDS in 1993, while living in France, where he had emigrated in 1960. As an editor in a publishing company, he helped bring Latin American literature to the attention of the European public.

11. For Villaverde, see the Medina interview, note 10.

12. Nancy Morejón, who identifies herself as an Afro-Caribbean woman, has lectured extensively throughout the United States. She lives in Cuba, where her continued work on the role of blacks in Cuban history and culture has established her as the authority on that subject.

13. See the interview with García.

.ː. .ː. .ː.

Bibliography

Alvarez, Julia. *How the García Girls Lost Their Accent*. Chapel Hill, North Carolina: Algonquin Books of Chapel Hill, 1991.

———. *In The Name of Salome*. Chapel Hill, North Carolina: Algonquin Books of Chapel Hill, 2000.

———. *Saving the World*. Chapel Hill, North Carolina: Algonquin Books of Chapel Hill, 2006.

Alvarez-Borland, Isabel. *Cuban-American Literature of Exile: From Person to Persona*. Charlottesville: University of Virginia Press, 2002.

Arenas, Reinaldo. *Before Night Falls*. New York: Viking, 1993.

Augenbraum, Harold, and Margarite Fernández Olmos, eds. *The Latino Reader: An American Literary Tradition from 1542 to the Present*. New York: Houghton Mifflin, 1997.

Benítez Rojo, Antonio. *The Repeating Island: The Caribbean and the Postmodern Perspective*, trans. James Maraniss. Durham, North Carolina: Duke University Press, 1996.

Blanco, Richard. *City of a Hundred Fires*. Pittsburgh: University of Pittsburgh Press, 1997.

———. *Directions to the Beach of the Dead*. Tucson: University of Arizona Press, 2005.

Bruce-Novoa, Juan. *Chicano Authors: Inquiry by Interviews*. Austin: The University of Texas Press, 1980.

Cabrera Infante, Guillermo. *Vista del amanecer en el trópico*. Barcelona: Editorial Seix Barral, 1974. Published in translation as *A View of Dawn in the Tropics*, trans. Suzanne Jill Levine. New York: Harper & Row, 1978.

Caminero-Santangelo, Marta. "Contesting the Boundaries of 'Exile' Latino/a Literature." *World Literature Today* 74, no. 3 (2000): 507–17.

Carpentier, Alejo. *El reino de este mundo*. Madrid: Alianza, 2006.

Casal, Lourdes, and Andrés R. Hernández. "Cubans in the U.S.: A Survey of the Literature." *Cuban Studies* 5 (1975): 25–52.

Castells, Ricardo. "Next Year in Cuba: Gustavo Pérez Firmat and the Rethinking of the Cuban-American Experience." *Secolas Annals* 30 (1999): 28–35.

Castillo, Sandra. *My Father Sings, To My Embarrassment*. Buffalo, New York: White Pine Press, 2002.

Christie, John S., and José Gonzalez, eds. *Latino Boom: An Anthology of U.S. Latino Literature*. New York: Pearson/Longman, 2005.

Christopherson, Bill. "Down from the Tower: Poetry as Confabulation." *Poetry* 179, no. 4 (2002): 217–25.

Cisneros, Sandra. *Loose Woman*. New York: Knopf, 1994.

———. *My Wicked, Wicked Ways*. New York: Turtle Bay Books, 1992.

Cortina, Rodolfo, ed. *Hispanic American Literature: An Anthology*. New York: NTC Publishing Group, 1998.

Cruz, Nilo. *Anna in the Tropics*. New York: Theatre Communications Group, 2003.

———. *Beauty of the Father*. New York: Theatre Communications Group, 2008.

———. *A Bicycle Country*. New York: Dramatists Play Service, 2004.

———. *Hortensia and the Museum of Dreams*. New York: Dramatists Play Service, 2004.

———. *Night Train to Bolina*. New York: Dramatists Play Service, 2004.

———. *Two Sisters and a Piano*. New York: Dramatists Play Service, 2004.

del Rio, Eduardo R. *The Prentice Hall Anthology of Latino Literature*. New York: Prentice Hall, 2002.

Eire, Carlos. *Waiting for Snow in Havana: The Confessions of a Cuban Boy*. New York: The Free Press/Simon & Schuster Inc., 2003.

Febles, Jorge. *Into the Mainstream: Essays on Spanish American and Latino Literature and Culture*. Newcastle, United Kingdom: Cambridge Scholars Publishing, 2006.

Fernández, Roberto. *Cuentos sin rumbos*. Miami, Florida: Ediciones Universal, 1975.

———. *En la ocho y la doce*. Boston: Houghton Mifflin, 2001.

———. *Holy Radishes!* Houston: Arte Público Press, 1995.

———. *La montaña rusa*. Houston: Arte Público Press, 1985.

———. *La vida es un special*. Miami: Ediciones Universal, 1981.

———. *Raining Backwards*. Houston: Arte Público Press, 1988.

Figueredo, Danilo H. "*Ser Cubano* (To Be Cuban): The Evolution of Cuban-American Literature." *Multicultural Review* 6, no. 1 (1997): 18–28.

Flora, Joseph M., Amber Vogel, and Bryan Albien Giemza, eds. *Southern Writers: A New Biographical Dictionary*. Baton Rouge: Louisiana State University Press, 2006.

García, Cristina. *The Agüero Sisters*. New York: Alfred A. Knopf, 1997.

———, ed. *Bordering Fires: The Vintage Book of Contemporary Mexican and Chicano and Chicana Literature*. New York: Vintage Books, 2006.

———, ed. *Cubanísimo: The Vintage Book of Contemporary Cuban Literature*. New York: Vintage Books, 2003.

——. *Dreaming in Cuban*. New York: Alfred A. Knopf, 1992.

——. *A Handbook to Luck*. New York: Alfred A. Knopf, 2007.

——. *Monkey Hunting*. New York: Alfred A. Knopf, 2003.

González, Celedonio. *Los cuatro embajadores*. Miami, Florida: Ediciones Universal, 1973.

——. *Los primos*. Miami, Florida: Ediciones Universal, 1971.

González, Ray, ed. *Currents from the Dancing River: Contemporary Latino Fiction, Nonfiction, and Poetry*. New York: Harcourt Brace, 1994.

Hernández, Carmen Dolores. *Puerto Rican Voices in English: Interviews with Writers*. Westport, Connecticut: Praeger, 1997.

Hijuelos, Oscar. *The Mambo Kings Play Songs of Love*. New York: Farrar, Straus, Giroux, 1989.

Horno-Delgado, Asunción, Eliana Ortega, Nina M. Scott, and Nancy Saporta Sternbach, eds. *Breaking Boundaries: Latina Writing and Critical Readings*. Amherst: University of Massachusetts Press, 1989.

Hospital, Carolina. *The Child of Exile: A Poetry Memoir*. Houston, Texas: Arte Público Press, 2004.

——, ed. *Cuban American Writers: Los Atrevidos*. Princeton: Ediciones Ellas, 1988.

——. "Heading to Havana," in *Naked Came the Manatee*. New York: Putnam, 1998.

—— and Jorge Cantera, eds. *A Century of Cuban Writers in Florida: Selected Prose and Poetry*. Sarasota, Florida: Pineapple Press, 1996.

—— and Carlos C. Medina. *A Little Love*. New York: Grand Central Publishing, 2000.

—— and Pablo Medina, trans. *Everyone Will Have to Listen: The Poetry of Tania Díaz*. Princeton: Ediciones Ella/Linden Lane Press, 1990.

Kandell, Jonathan. "Miami: City of Exiles," *Cigar Aficionado* 8, no. 5 (July/August 2000). Available at http://www.cigaraficionado.com/Cigar/CA_Archives/CA_Show_Article/0,2322,263,00.html (last accessed on January 8, 2008).

Kanellos, Nicolás, ed. *Biographical Dictionary of Hispanic Literature in the United States: The Literature of Puerto Ricans, Cuban Americans, and Other Hispanic Writers*. New York: Greenwood Press, 1989.

——. *Herencia: The Anthology of Hispanic Literature in the United States*. New York: Oxford University Press, 2001.

Laviera, Tato. *La Carreta Made a U-Turn*. Gary, Indiana: Arte Público Press, 1979.

Lezama Lima, José. *Oppiano Licario*. Mexico City: Ediciones Era, 1977.

——. *Paradiso*. Havana: UNEAC, 1966.

López, Iraida. ". . . And There Is Only My Imagination Where Our History Should Be: An Interview with Cristina Garcia." In *Bridges to Cuba/Puentes a Cuba* edited by Ruth Behar, 102-114. Ann Arbor: University of Michigan Press, 1995.

Luis, William. *Dance Between Two Cultures: Latino Caribbean Literature Written in the United States*. Nashville, Tennessee: Vanderbilt University Press, 1997.

Machado, Eduardo. *Broken Eggs*. New York: Samuel French, 2004.

——. *The Cook: A Play*. New York: Samuel French, 2004.

——. *The Floating Island Plays*. New York: Theatre Communications Group, 1991.

——. *Kissing Fidel*. New York: Samuel French, 2006.

——. *The Modern Ladies of Guanabacoa*. New York: Theatre Communications Group, 1983.

——. *Once Removed*. New York: Theatre Communications Group, 1988.

—— and Michael Domitrovich. *Tastes Like Cuba: An Exile's Hunger for Home*. New York: Gotham, 2007.

Mackie, Patrick. "The Low Style." *Critical Quarterly* 42, no. 4 (2000): 30.

Mañach, Jorge. *Martí, el Apóstol*. Madrid: Espasa-Calpe, 1933.

Martínez, Dionisio. *Bad Alchemy: Poems*. New York: W. W. Norton, 1995.

——. *Climbing Back: Poems*. New York: W. W. Norton, 2001.

——. *Dancing at the Chelsea*. Brockport, New York: State Street Press, 1992.

——. *History as a Second Language*. Columbus: Ohio State University Press, 1993.

Medina, Pablo. *Arching into the Afterlife*. Tempe, Arizona: Bilingual Press/Editorial Bilingüe, 1991.

——. *The Cigar Roller*. New York: Grove Press, 2005.

——. *Exiled Memories: A Cuban Childhood*. New York: Persea Books, 2002. First published by University of Texas Press, 1990.

——. *The Floating Island*. Buffalo, N.Y.: White Pine Press, 1999.

——. *The Marks of Birth*. New York: Farrar, Straus and Giroux, 1994.

——. *Points of Balance/Puntos de apoyo*. New York City: Four Way Books; Hanover, New Hampshire: University Press of New England, 2005.

——. *Pork Rind and Cuban Songs*. Washington: Nuclassics and Science Pub. Co., 1975.

——. *Puntos de apoyo*. Madrid: Editorial Betania, 2002.

——. *The Return of Felix Nogara*. New York: Persea Books, 2000.

—— and Carolina Hospital, trans. *Everyone Will Have to Listen: The Poetry of Tania Díaz*. Princeton: Ediciones Ella/Linden Lane Press, 1990.

Menéndez, Ana. *In Cuba I Was a German Shepherd*. New York: Grove Press, 2001.

——. *Loving Ché*. New York: Grove Press, 2003.

Milián, Alberto. "Defying Time and History: An Interview with Ricardo Pau-Llosa." *Manoa* 15, no. 1 (2003): 141–51. Available at http://www.nd.edu/%7Endr/issues/ndr13/paullosa/paullosa.html (last accessed on January 8, 2008).

Montes Huidobro, Matías. *Desterrados al Fuego*. Mexico City: Fondo de Cultura Económica, 1975.

Morejón, Nancy. *Paisaje célebre*. Caracas, Venezuela: Fundarte, 1993.

Mormino, Gary Ross, and George E. Pozzetta. *The Immigrant World of Ybor City: Italians and Their Latin Neighbors in Tampa, 1885–1985.* Gainesville: University Press of Florida, 1998.

Obejas, Achy. *Days of Awe.* New York: Ballantine Books, 2001.

———, ed. *Havana Noir.* New York: Akashic Books, 2007.

———. *Memory Mambo.* Pittsburgh, Pennsylvania: Cleis Press, 1996.

———. *This Is What Happened in Our Other Life.* Berkeley: Small Press Distribution, 2007.

———. *We Came All the Way from Cuba So You Could Dress Like This?* Pittsburgh, Pennsylvania: Cleis Press, 1994.

Pacheco, Ferdie. *Ybor City Chronicles: A Memoir.* Gainesville: University Press of Florida, 1994.

Padilla, Heberto. *Fuera del juego.* 2nd ed. Mexico City: Universidad Autónoma del Estado de México, 1982.

Pau-Llosa, Ricardo. *Bread of the Imagined.* Tempe, Arizona: Bilingual Press/ Editorial Bilingüe, 1992.

———. *Cuba.* New York: Carnegie Mellon, 1993.

———. *The Hollow.* New York: Carnegie Mellon, 1999.

———. *The Mastery Impulse.* New York: Carnegie Mellon, 2003.

———. *Parable Hunter.* New York: Carnegie Mellon, 2008.

———. *Sorting Metaphors.* Tallahassee, Florida: Anhinga Press, 1983.

———. *Un acercamiento a Polesello.* Translated from the English by the author. Buenos Aires, Argentina: Ediciones de Arte Gaglianone, 1984.

———. *Vereda Tropical.* New York: Carnegie Mellon, 1999.

Pérez Firmat, Gustavo. *Anything But Love.* Houston, Texas: Arte Público Press, 2000.

———. *Bilingual Blues.* Tempe, Arizona: Bilingual Press/Editorial Bilingüe, 1995.

———. "Carolina Cuban." In *Triple Crown: Chicano, Puerto Rican, and Cuban-American Poetry,* edited by Roberto Durán, Judith Ortiz Cofer, and Gustavo Pérez Firmat, 121–167. Bilingual Press/Editorial Bilingüe, 1987.

———. *Cincuenta lecciones de exilio y desexilio.* Miami, Florida: Ediciones Universal, 2000.

———. *The Cuban Condition: Translation and Identity in Modern Cuban Literature.* New York: Cambridge University Press, 1989.

———. *Do the Americas Have a Common Literature?* Durham, North Carolina: Duke University Press, 1990.

———. *Equivocaciones.* Madrid: Editorial Betania, 1989.

———. *Idle Fictions: The Hispanic Vanguard Novel, 1926–1934.* Durham, North Carolina: Duke University Press, 1982.

———. *Life on the Hyphen: The Cuban-American Way.* Austin: University of Texas Press, 1994.

———. *Literature and Liminality: Festive Readings in the Hispanic Tradition.* Durham, North Carolina: Duke University Press, 1986.

———. *My Own Private Cuba: Essays on Cuban Literature and Culture*. Boulder, Colorado: Society of Spanish and Spanish-American Studies, 1999.

———. *Next Year in Cuba*. New York: Anchor Books, 1995.

———. *Scar Tissue*. Tempe, Arizona: Bilingual Press/Editorial Bilingüe, 2005.

———. *Tongue Ties: Logo-Eroticism in Anglo-Hispanic Literature*. New York: Palgrave Macmillan, 2003.

———. *Vidas en vilo: La cultura cubanoamericana*. Madrid: Colibrí Editorial, 2000.

Prida, Dolores. *Beautiful Señoritas and Other Plays*. Edited and introduced by Judith Weiss. Houston, Texas: Arte Público Press, 1991.

Rivero, Eliana. "From Immigrants to Ethnics: Cuban Women Writers in the U.S." In *Breaking Boundaries: Latina Writing and Critical Readings*, edited by Asunción Horno-Delgado, Eliana Ortega, Nina M. Scott, and Nancy Saporta Sternbach, 189–200. Amherst: University of Massachusetts Press, 1989.

———. "Hispanic Literature in the United States: Self-Image and Conflict." *Revista Chicano-Riqueña* 13, nos. 3–4 (1985): 173–91.

Rosales, Guillermo. *La casa de los náufragos*. Madrid: Ediciones Siruela, 2003.

Smorkaloff, Pamela Maria. *Cuban Writers on and off the Island*. New York: Twayne Publishers, 1999.

Stavans, Ilan. *Spanglish: The Making of a New American Language*. New York: Rayo, 2004.

Suárez, Virgil. *90 Miles: Selected and New Poems*. Pittsburgh, Pennsylvania, 2005.

———. *Banyan: Poems*. Baton Rouge: Louisiana State University Press. 2001.

———. *The Cutter: A Novel*. New York: Available Press, 1991.

———. *Garabato Poems*. San Antonio: Wings Press, 1998.

———. *Going Under: A Novel*. Houston: Arte Público Press, 1996.

———. *Guide to the Blue Tongue: Poems*. Urbana: University of Illinois Press, 2002.

———. *Havana Thursdays: A Novel*. Houston: Arte Público Press, 1995.

———. *In the Republic of Longing: Poems*. Tempe, Arizona: Bilingual Press/Editorial Bilingüe, 2000.

———. *Infinite Refuge*. Houston: Arte Público Press, 2002.

———. *Latin Jazz*. New York: W. Morrow, 1989.

———. *Palm Crows*. Tucson: University of Arizona Press, 2001.

———. *Spared Angola: Memories from a Cuban-American Childhood*. Houston: Arte Público Press, 1997.

———. *Welcome to the Oasis and Other Stories*. Houston: Arte Público Press, 1992.

———. *You Come Singing*. Lake View Terrace, California: Tía Chucha Press, 1998.

———, and Delia Poey. *Iguana Dreams: New Latino Fiction*. New York: HarperPerennial, 1993.

——, and Ryan G. Van Cleave, eds. *American Diaspora*. Iowa City: University of Iowa Press, 2001.

——, and Ryan G. Van Cleave, eds. *Landscapes and Dreams*. Hammond, Louisiana: Louisiana Literature Press, 2003.

——, and Ryan G. Van Cleave, eds. *Vespers: Contemporary American Poems of Religion and Spirituality*. Iowa City: University of Iowa Press, 2003.

Valero, Roberto. *Este viento de cuaresma*. Miami, Florida: Ediciones Universal, 1994.

Viera, Joseph M. "Matriarchy and Mayhem: Awakenings in Cristina García's *Dreaming in Cuban*." *The Americas Review* 24, no. 3 (1996): 231–42.

Yglesias, José. *Guns in the Closet*. Houston, Texas: Arte Público Press, 1996.

——. *A Wake in Ybor City*. New York: Holt, Rinehart and Winston, 1963.

·:· ·:· ·:·

About the Author

Eduardo R. del Rio was born in Havana, Cuba, in 1960 and has lived in exile in the United States since the age of four. He received his Ph.D. from Texas A&M University in 1996 and is now an associate professor of English at the University of Texas at Brownsville. His essays have appeared in national and international peer-reviewed journals, and he is the editor of *The Prentice Hall Anthology of Latino Literature*. His most recent article appears in the collection *Into the Mainstream: Essays on Spanish American and Latino Literature and Culture* edited by Jorge Febles. In 2004, the National Endowment for the Humanities awarded him a Faculty Research Grant so that he could interview the authors in this volume.

Library of Congress Cataloging-in-Publication Data

One island, many voices : conversations with
Cuban-American writers / Eduardo R. del Rio.
p. cm.
Includes bibliographical references.
ISBN 978-0-8165-2714-4 (alk. paper)—
ISBN 978-0-8165-2806-6 (pbk. : alk. paper)
1. American literature—Cuban American authors—
Interviews. 2. Cuban Americans—Intellectual life.
I. Rio, Eduardo del, 1960–
PS508.C83O54   2008
810.8'8687291—dc22   2008018872